Candy Making for Beginners

Candy Making

for Beginners

Easy Recipes for Homemade Caramels, Gummies, Lollipops, and More

Karen Neugebauer

PHOTOGRAPHY BY MARIJA VIDAL

callisto publishing
an imprint of Sourcebooks

Published by Callisto Publishing LLC C/O Sourcebooks LLC
P.O. Box 4410, Naperville, Illinois 60567-4410
(630) 961-3900
callistopublishing.com

Printed and bound in China
OGP 2

TO THE KID INSIDE US ALL.
MAY THEY BE LET OUT TO
PLAY MORE OFTEN!

Contents

Introduction

CANDY IS ONE OF LIFE'S GREAT EQUALIZERS. It's there for us in good times and bad. It's the lollipop after a doctor's visit or the bowl of candy waiting for you at the bank teller's counter. You'll find a chocolate mint on the pillow of a freshly made hotel bed and another on top of the bill when visiting your favorite restaurant. The Tooth Fairy might leave a few candy coins in exchange for a lost baby tooth, just as a doctor might give you a sucker after a visit. Candy communicates something truly elemental. It reminds us that life can be sweet, even as we're enduring its unavoidable annoyances.

Candy marks moments, big and small. Throwing a kid's birthday party? You're going to need some wrapped goodies for the piñata. Meeting a friend's new baby? That's a good excuse to shop for bonbons. Someone graduates. A promotion at work. Going to the movies. Even checking out at the grocery store. Candy is there.

Candy has always been a part of life. Sweet treats have been lifting our spirits since ancient times, when the Greeks and Egyptians valued honey as medicine and referred to it as the ambrosia of the gods. Native Americans developed maple syrup and candy, and many of their traditions came to revolve around maple sugaring season.

Candy brings holidays to life. In fact, it's hard to imagine any holiday without candy. Halloween would not be the same without trick-or-treating. No one would search for plastic eggs without the promise of jellybeans and chocolate robin's eggs inside. And kids would sleep in all December long were it not for Advent calendars, peppermint bark, and stocking stuffers. All the rituals, moments, and shared experiences are just better with candy. In many homes, cooking candy is as synonymous with the holidays as the smell of freshly fallen leaves, fires in the hearth, mulled cider, and the scent of evergreen trees inside the home. The aroma of family recipes wafting through the house is like a sensory time machine back to childhood. For younger generations, those sweet scents mean it's a special time. It's time to make the candy!

Many people think making candy at home, in your own kitchen, is complicated, difficult, and expensive. It's not. Getting started requires only basic ingredients, a few pieces of common equipment, and some heat. That's it. With just a little effort, you'll be able to take your holidays to a whole new level. Birthdays, anniversaries, and thank-you gifts will be that much more memorable when you add the personal touch of homemade candy crafted with love. Plus, there is a great deal of joy that comes from creating something delicious with your own hands. Your creations become an expression of you.

Your candy can be soft or hard, chewy or sticky, smooth or chalky, fluffy or dense, or simply dissolve the moment it hits your tongue. It can be sweet or savory or both and include everything from nuts and seeds to fruits, liquors, creams, and spices. You can make soft candy, like caramels and Pâte de Fruit, hard candy, like toffee and lollipops, or chewy candy, like taffy and gumdrops. Imagine the exciting combinations just waiting to be discovered!

Candy making is a great way to spend quality time getting creative (and sticky) with family and friends. It's a lot of fun, it's delicious, and most importantly, it just makes life that much sweeter.

PÂTE DE FRUIT, page 110

It's Candy Time

THESE DAYS MOST CANDY COMES FROM GIANT factories using secret recipes and questionable ingredients. But it wasn't always so. Candy, like any food, has a long tradition of being lovingly created by someone in the home, with recipes passed down from one generation to the next. These treasured recipes called for special tools, specific techniques, and even secret ingredients. While some of this still holds true, the mystery behind candy making has been dispelled so that with a few key pieces of knowledge, you, too, can make wonderfully tasty candies in your kitchen like a pro.

In the chapters that follow, we'll break down the various categories, like barks and fudge, lollipops and hard candy, and more. Here, we'll focus on the basics you need to get started with your candy experiments.

Key Equipment & Tools

You probably have most of the items you need to launch your candy kitchen, such as pots, pans, bowls, and spoons. A few tools, however, require careful thought and a solid working knowledge of how they function when preparing candy.

Kitchen scale. Unlike using measuring cups and spoons with baking, it is often important to weigh ingredients (including liquids) when making candy. Kitchen scales are readily available online and can be very inexpensive (often $15 or less). Look for a digital scale that can handle up to 11 pounds (5kg) and has an accuracy (resolution) of 1 or 2 grams. Candy making relies on precise chemical reactions that can only happen with the right ratio of ingredients at the start. You will always get better and more consistent results when you weigh ingredients.

Heavy-bottomed saucepans are a must. They spread the heat out and help avoid burning from the hotspots common with lower-quality cookware. The most useful sizes of pots are the 2-quart (small) and the 4-quart (large). Stainless steel is best, but most high-quality nonstick pots will do the job. Avoid the ones with ridges on the inside. Avoid aluminum pots. Aluminum reacts with acid and baking soda and can impart an unpleasant metallic aftertaste.

Candy thermometers are extremely important, as many candies require cooking to very precise temperatures. I recommend digital thermometers. They are easier to read and are more precise. Analog thermometers come in two versions: (1) a metal probe with a dial at the top or (2) a glass rod with mercury inside. Both have disadvantages. The metal probe and dial versions are often inaccurate and can show temperature changes too slowly. And glass mercury thermometers can break, releasing poison and sharp glass. Also, with this version, the temperatures printed on the side scrub off over time. With any thermometer, you must check for accuracy. To do so, simply boil water and take the temperature in the middle of the pot without touching the bottom. The temperature should read 212°F (100°C). If it doesn't, you will need to calibrate it. The boiling point of water if you live close to sea level is 212°F (100°C). If you live at higher altitudes, the boiling point decreases by 0.9°F (0.5°C) for every 500-foot (150-meter) increase in altitude. Atmospheric pressure decreases as you move higher. You could look up the boiling point of water where you live, but it's easier to simply

boil water and take a measurement. This method takes into account both your altitude and any variation in your thermometer. If, say, your thermometer reads 209°F, just remember to subtract 3°F when you use it.

High-heat spatulas are specially designed to handle heat over 400°F (204.4°C). Candy syrups need to cook to 300°F or higher, and everyday spatulas will simply melt. Also, since we use them for stirring, not flipping, we will refer to them as **stir sticks.** Wooden stir sticks are an option, but I don't recommend them. Wood can be hard to clean, and it contains many grooves where moisture and bacteria like to hide.

Oven mitts or pot holders are a simple, common, yet crucial piece of equipment necessary for dealing with pot handles that get very hot, especially when pouring. Be sure you have suitable protection on hand because burns can really sour one's love of making candy.

Baking sheets with sides are just like standard baking sheets but with a raised lip on all four sides, about 1 inch high. Look for stainless steel half sheet pans, as the full sheet pan may not fit your oven. You only need one or two. These are often also called rimmed baking or cookie sheets.

Parchment paper and silicone baking mats for pouring out toffee and other candies. Silicone baking mats are my preference. Buy two or more mats that fit a standard half sheet pan. Parchment paper is good for lining baking sheets, but the paper is very thin and can easily roll and tear, which can be frustrating.

Silicone molds are handy for forming cute shapes and maintaining uniform pieces. Avoid plastic molds, as these will stick and could easily melt.

Low-watt microwaves are best for chocolate and candy work. The recipes in this book were written for a 1000-watt microwave. Check your microwave before cooking and adjust the power accordingly. For example, if you are using a 2000-watt microwave, set the power to 50%.

Glass mixing bowls are crucial. Clear Pyrex is preferable. They're dishwasher and microwave safe, they don't break easily, and you can see the contents. Plus, they hold their temperature longer, which is important when working with chocolate or barks. Start with two 1.5-quart bowls (small), two 2.5-quart bowls (medium), and one 4-quart bowl (large). You also might want to pick up a bunch of little prep bowls (3.5 x 1.5 inches) for premeasuring your smaller ingredients separately like a professional!

Pizza cutters and knives. One pizza cutter, one standard chef's knife, one paring knife, and one serrated knife (bread knife) will do just about all the cutting and scoring when making candy. Metal knives are far superior. Avoid ceramic knives completely because they chip easily with candy work.

Dipping forks are quite useful for coating truffles or toffee pieces in chocolate. Most common are two-prong forks for truffle squares, three-prong forks for dipping larger pieces like toffee diamonds or peppermint patties, and circle forks for dipping rolled truffles. Look for ones with wooden handles, as they are much easier to hold.

Key Ingredients

Quality ingredients are, of course, very important when cooking anything. Most companies mass-producing candy use the cheapest ingredients possible because it makes them the largest profit. We're in the business of making deliciousness, not profits. So, it goes without saying, buy the best ingredients you can get your hands on.

Beyond that obvious point, when making candy, you will constantly come across the same few ingredients, so it's important to be familiar with them.

Sugar is probably the key ingredient in candy. The second-most important benefit of cooking with sugar is that it's a preservative (the first is its yumminess, of course). Bacteria need water to grow. Thus, the more water in a given food, the quicker it will spoil. Candy is shelf-stable, meaning it won't spoil quickly, since the primary ingredient is sugar and much of the water is boiled out in the cooking process. Soft candies have more water and, therefore, shorter shelf lives compared with hard candies, which can be safe to eat for many years if stored in a dry environment.

For the purpose of this book, sugar as an ingredient refers to granulated C&H Pure Cane Sugar (white table sugar). Most confectioners agree that cane sugar is preferable to beet sugar, an ingredient found in less-expensive brands. Even though the chemical structures of both sugars are the same, cane sugar just seems to work better. If you prefer more natural sugars, consider turbinado, demerara, muscovado, or raw/less processed types. However, keep in mind that you won't get the same results if you substitute one kind of sugar for another.

Brown sugar is similar to white sugar, except it's less processed and contains molasses. The darker the sugar, the more molasses. Confectioners' sugar, also known as icing sugar, 10X, or powdered sugar, is finely ground white sugar with a bit of added cornstarch to prevent clumping.

Sugar syrups are typically a mixture of two simple sugars, glucose and fructose, sometimes known as invert sugars. Candy makers use them to stop crystals from forming during both the cooking and the cooling process. It's a good idea to try out any recipe a couple of times exactly to get a good sense of what is happening during the cooking process. With that knowledge in hand, you'll be able to successfully swap out either glucose or corn syrup with other syrups (like honey) and really begin experimenting on your own. Without a good grasp of how the chemical reactions can vary, you might be left with candy that won't get hard, has a weird texture, or burns before it can reach critical temperature zones.

Glucose is very useful for avoiding cloudiness or browning in hard candies like lollipops. It browns at very high temperatures, making it easier to work with than other liquid sweeteners. If you have concerns about gluten allergies, be sure to check the label. Glucose can contain a variety of ingredients, including wheat, but that is more common in Europe. In the US, we mostly use corn (we grow a lot of corn here) or other starchy substances like rice or potato. Corn syrup can be a substitute for glucose if wheat is a concern, though browning is a risk.

Some of the recipes in this book use corn syrup. Corn syrup has a ratio of about 45% glucose to 55% fructose. This helps achieve the Maillard reactions you sometimes want with things like caramels. Maillard reactions give caramels that characteristic complex toasted flavor and lovely creamy brown color. While corn syrup is similar to granulated C&H Pure Cane Sugar in its makeup, it is NOT the same as high-fructose corn syrup! Table sugar (sucrose) is 50% glucose and 50% fructose. High-fructose corn syrup is a lot sweeter by design, sometimes having 90% fructose and only 10% glucose. It is overly sweet and can take away from the overall flavor balance of candy. For this reason, you should avoid it.

Fructose is about twice as sweet as C&H Pure Cane Sugar and is found naturally in fruits. This type of sugar browns and burns quickly when cooking. This can be a good thing when making caramels, but it's annoying when making hard candy. Honey, molasses, maple syrup, and agave syrup all have lots of fructose but won't typically provide the same quality results as glucose and corn syrup.

Water is an important ingredient when cooking candy, and the quality of your water matters. Filtered water is generally preferable to tap water. If the water tastes good and clean, then your product will taste good and clean as well. Avoid water with minerals or a heavy, stale taste or scent.

Butter and cream are primarily for making toffee, caramels, and fudge. The butter coats the sugar crystals and gives that characteristic mouthfeel. All the recipes in this book that call for cream need heavy whipping cream (contains 40% fat) for the recipe to work correctly. Do not use light whipping cream or half-and-half, as the fat content is not high enough to get the correct mouthfeel. I generally use salted butter for my recipes because it is the easiest to get and I prefer the taste. If you are using unsalted butter, you can add a small pinch of salt (about ⅓ teaspoon) per ½ cup of butter, but it is not necessary for the recipe to work if you prefer less salt.

Gelatin gives marshmallows a puffy texture and gives gummies a stretchy, soft, and wiggly bite. It comes in powders or sheets. Be careful, though, as the kind of gelatin you use matters, too. Different types work differently. I highly recommend using powdered gelatin, as rehydrating it is simple and powdered gelatin is easy to measure out in small amounts. Gelatin sheets can be used instead, but they take longer to hydrate, are less readily available, and can be harder to measure out in small amounts, so I don't recommend them for beginners.

Acids are common in candy making, especially tartaric, malic, and citric acids. They are responsible for the tart, lemony flavor in lemon drops and the face-puckering sour sensation in sour gummies. Remember that a little goes a long way, and make sure you are using only food-grade versions.

Salt is an essential ingredient that helps balance flavors in certain candies. Salt provides a wonderful contrast to sugar and gives you that tempting salty-and-sweet combination we've all succumbed to at one time or another.

Flavorings are important, and you can choose what you like best. Vanilla extract is very common in caramels, fudge, and marshmallows. Other popular flavors such as cherry, grape, apple, and butterscotch are common in hard candy. Flavor sets will give you more options for experimenting and are often less expensive than buying flavorings separately.

Colors make hard candies so much more attractive and are a good indication of what flavor to expect. Colors come in liquid drops, powders, or gels. I recommend liquid drops for hard candy, as they are the easiest to measure and mix in. Alternatively, many liquids, such as juices, already have a color built in.

Cocoa powder is mostly for making fudge. It comes in a natural version or in a darker one. Natural cocoa powder is lighter and contains more cocoa butter fat. Dutch cocoa is darker because it is processed with an alkali to reduce the acidity and harshness of the cacao and to remove even more of the cocoa butter fat. This is an important distinction in baking recipes, but either will work well for most basic candy recipes.

Chocolate is often mistaken for a candy because of the sugar it contains, but it's not candy at all. Chocolate is naturally shelf-stable, as it has almost no water in it. Added sugar is only for flavor purposes, not as a way to keep chocolate from spoiling.

Chocolate Basics

The world of chocolate is exploding. The quality and available flavors we're seeing in the marketplace now are quite amazing. With so many options, it can seem daunting to select the right chocolate to use in a given recipe. But the good news is that it's pretty easy to make the right choice when you know what to look for.

Dark chocolate is like a fine wine. Its many wonderful flavors spring naturally from the bean itself and can change dramatically depending on the soil and climate where it was grown.

Dark chocolate is comprised of cocoa mass (ground-up cacao beans) and sugar but may also contain additional cocoa butter, an emulsifier (such as soy lecithin) to keep the texture smooth, and often also vanilla. Typically, dark chocolate has between 60% and 85% cocoa content, but this can vary drastically. Chocolate that is labeled "extra dark" or "bittersweet" generally has 70% to 85% cocoa and will be on the bitter side. Semisweet chocolate contains more sugar, with cocoa percentages typically in the 60% to 70% range. Whatever percentage you choose, be sure to taste the chocolate to make sure you actually enjoy that particular flavor. If you bought 20 different bars, all with 70% cocoa content, they all might taste different from one another, and whichever you use will change the flavor of the confection that you are making. It's fun to experiment with the different makers, origins, and percentages as well as combining a few to make something new.

Unsweetened chocolate is made from ground-up beans only. No sugar is added, so it has 100% cocoa content. Technically, 100% cocoa is not legally considered chocolate because chocolate must contain at least 1% sugar. However, you don't need to worry about arbitrary legal definitions. The lack of sugar in unsweetened chocolate does not change how it will temper or handle when you cook with it.

Milk chocolate is the most common worldwide. The cocoa content typically ranges from 30% to 45%, and it contains the same ingredients as dark chocolate but with the addition of milk powder. The milk powder displaces part of the cocoa mass in the chocolate, so the result tastes sweeter, creamier, and less bitter.

White chocolate is just like milk chocolate, but it is sweeter and has a cream color due to its lack of cocoa solids (the stuff that makes chocolate brown). White chocolate is a great choice for butter truffles or for adding decoration to milk or dark chocolate treats. White chocolate follows the rules of regular chocolate when it comes to mouthfeel/texture, flavor delivery, and workability, due to its high cocoa butter content. However, plenty of fake white chocolates exist out there. Look for cocoa butter to be one of the first two ingredients on the label. Legitimate white chocolate contains at least 20% cocoa butter, but look for the varieties that have closer to 30% cocoa butter, as they are much smoother, have a cleaner flavor, and are more user-friendly.

Coating chocolate, also known as almond bark, is not actually chocolate. It contains palm-kernel oil instead of cocoa butter. This is often called "fake" or "imitation" chocolate. You'll find it's the sweetest of all the options, and, generally, candy cooks use it because it's inexpensive and doesn't require tempering. Almond bark is great for kid treats and as a backup plan if tempering is not your thing.

Chocolate brands to look for include Gusto Chocolates, Volta Craft Chocolate, Felchlin, Valrhona, Scharffen Berger, and Forte Chocolates.

Weather & Candy

Candy is hygroscopic, meaning it will absorb moisture (water) from its surroundings. This is why a nice hard candy will get all soggy and squishy over time with just regular humidity in the air. When making candy, we are trying to reach the water-sugar balance necessary to create the texture we're looking to achieve. For example, a brittle is hard because it contains very little water, whereas a chewy caramel is softer because of its higher moisture content. After cooking, all candies will start to reabsorb moisture, pulling it out of the air. That's why it's harder making candy on hot and humid days. Working in an air-conditioned kitchen or running a dehumidifier can help a lot. Keep in mind that the moisture in the kitchen is all that really matters. It can be raining and cold outside, as long as the humidity is low in the kitchen. If you run into trouble, get yourself a wall thermometer to indicate the humidity level. They're quite common and easy to find online. Candy making is best in the 35% to 40% humidity range, with room temperatures between 66°F and 72°F.

The Safe Confectioner

Boiling sugar syrup can be very dangerous if one lacks the proper respect. It is imperative to be safe when making candy. First, always use pot holders, oven mitts, or handle sleeves when touching a pot. The handles get extremely hot, and heat can travel through thinner protective layers when you're pouring candy slowly into molds. Second, use nitrile or neoprene gloves. They help keep you clean, and you can quickly remove them if you spill burning-hot candy on your hand. Last, but certainly not least, measure out your ingredients into small bowls beforehand. With everything ready to go, you won't be running around frantically measuring ingredients over boiling pots. Staying organized will go a long way in keeping you safe.

TIGER STRIPES BARK, page 22

Barks & Fudge

BARKS AND FUDGE ARE BOTH DELICIOUS AND EASY to customize, which is probably why they are among the most common chocolate-like confections for the newbie home candy cook.

Barks

Barks are popular, easy to make, and able to accept just about any combination of dried fruits and nuts you have on hand. The mix of fruit, nuts, and seeds is beautiful, especially when the colors contrast with the chocolate. There is a certain attractiveness to the chaos of a bark. Broken pieces with rough edges and an unruly scattering of toppings provide a feast for the eyes. Somehow, the more wild and uneven the scattering of toppings, the more desirable the bark.

KEYS TO SUCCESS

- Tasting the almond bark (coating chocolate) is important. Every brand is different. If you are good at tempering, feel free to use actual chocolate for any of the recipes instead.

- When picking out toppings, look for ingredients that regularly pair well together and have complementary colors, contrasting textures, and binge-worthy flavors (like salty and sweet).

- Spread the almond bark thin (about ¼ inch is best) and get your toppings on quickly, as the bark/chocolate always seems to set faster than you want. A simple trick is to put a slightly warm towel (no hotter than body temperature) between your counter and baking sheet to prevent a cool counter from speeding up the setting process.

- Tuck away your perfectionist side and be wild when distributing toppings. Whatever random mess you create will become a big part of what makes your bark beautiful.

- Lightly tap down toppings so they are sure to stick to the bark instead of falling off.

- Let your bark set fully prior to breaking it up. If you decide to put your bark in the refrigerator, cover it with parchment paper first and leave it in for no more than 20 minutes. Resist the urge to remove the parchment paper until the bark returns to room temperature, about 20 minutes. If you expose the cool bark to the warm air, condensation will cover your beautiful creation with moisture and draw the sugar out of the fruit and almond bark. This whitish layer over everything is called a sugar bloom, and it imparts an unappealing sandpaper texture to your creations.

Fudge

The ideal fudge is like a white whale—mythical, elusive, and obsession-inducing to the point of madness in some. It's creamy yet firm. It must melt in your mouth in just the right way, yet no one can quite describe that way except to say you'll know it when you experience it. One of my favorite gifts I received as an adult is an elegant crystal candy dish from my grandma, Janet Stiles. Not only was it precious and thoughtful because candy holds a special place in my heart, but when I opened the domed lid, it was filled with a fresh batch of perfectly made fudge. To this day, I have never made (or eaten) a batch of fudge as good as hers. She set the bar very high! Truly great fudge like hers is imbued with tiny, barely discernible sugar crystals. The real trick to achieving this almost intangible state of perfection lies not in the ingredients or even in the cooking . . . it's in the stirring. And if that wasn't Zen enough, part of mastering this technique is knowing when not to stir. The process goes like this: Stir the sugar, cream, and cocoa powder to combine well. Boil the mixture without stirring. Let it cool to about 130°F without disturbing it. Then, and only then, stir vigorously until a dull, matte sheen is visible. Finally, let the mixture cool completely. In simpler terms: Stirring while cool leads to smaller crystals, and stirring while hot leads to larger crystals, so only stir when the fudge is on the cooler side, which happens both at the beginning and at the end.

KEYS TO SUCCESS

- Use medium heat only; high heat can easily scorch the fudge and cause it to quickly boil over.

- Eliminate any remaining sugar crystals by washing down the sides of the pot with water and a pastry brush.

- To get the creamiest texture, once you start stirring at the end, commit! Don't stop until the mixture turns dull (matte). Use a hand beater if your arm is not up to the task.

- Mix in nuts and other inclusions right before pouring into the dish or sprinkle on top and press into the fudge once it's poured out.

Technique Spotlight
HOW TO PROPERLY MELT BARK AND CHOCOLATE

People wonder why chocolate is so hard to melt without burning. This simple question has a very complex answer. For our purposes, we'll focus on one of the main reasons: Chocolate and bark are thick, with particles packed together very tightly. This means that while the outer layers may have melted, the inner layers often remain solid. It's easy to overheat and burn the outside while waiting for the inside to melt. The solution is to melt both bark and chocolate slowly.

METHOD 1: MICROWAVE

Microwaves cook from the inside by boiling what little water is in bark and chocolate. The boiling causes the water molecules to move against their surroundings, causing friction and producing heat. This is why it is extremely important to only heat with a microwave in short intervals. In between cooking, remove the bowl and stir or press down on the chunks of bark and chocolate, even if they appear unchanged. This will redistribute the water molecules and expose new pieces to the surface of the bowl as it heats up.

METHOD 2: DOUBLE BOILER

While this technique has been in practice for quite some time, it does have significant drawbacks. The steam from the water in the pot below increases moisture in the air, which neither barks nor chocolate appreciate, resulting in thicker flow (higher viscosity). In addition, water accumulates on the bottom of the bowl and may easily find its way into the bark or chocolate while pouring. Wiping the bowl down is good, but even one drop of water can spoil the entire batch. This is known as seizing, which can turn silky smooth bark or chocolate into a cement-like blob very quickly. Bottom line: Melt bark and chocolate in the microwave. It's easier, more likely to get the results you're looking for, and faster, too.

Trusty Cupboard Fruit & Nut Bark

PREP TIME: 5 minutes | **WORKING TIME:** 15 minutes | **SETTING TIME:** 15 minutes

YIELD: 2 POUNDS

As a parent of five kids, I am often expected to contribute a snack or dessert to some kind of school function, gathering, or sporting event. Any parent can relate. Inevitably, despite best intentions, some minor crisis erupts. It involves shoes or pets or broken toys or missing homework or whatever. The list is endlessly varied, but the results are always the same. You find yourself with precious few minutes remaining and nary a delicious homemade treat in sight. When this happens to you, relax. Here's a beautiful bark recipe that takes less than 40 minutes to make. It's delicious, and no one will ever know you made it at the last minute. Just be sure to keep a supply of almond bark on hand.

EQUIPMENT:

- Knife and cutting board
- Medium glass mixing bowl
- Stir stick
- Silicone baking mat

1 cup (150 grams) chopped dried fruit

24 ounces (680 grams) almond bark (white, milk, or dark)

1 or 2 pinches salt

1 cup (130 grams) nuts

1 ounce (28 grams) almond bark for drizzle (a different type from the main one, if possible)

1. Chop the fruit into small pieces. Skip this step if your fruit is the size of raisins or smaller.

2. Break up and slowly melt the 24 ounces of almond bark in a medium glass mixing bowl in the microwave in 20-second intervals, stirring briefly in between cooking. Repeat until all the pieces are fully melted. Make sure the almond bark does not get too hot, or it will burn.

3. Pour out onto a silicone baking mat or parchment-lined baking sheet and spread into an even, thin layer.

4. Sprinkle the salt evenly across the entire surface, then quickly repeat with the nuts and fruit.

5. Melt the remaining almond bark and drizzle over everything. Let set on the counter until firm. Break into pieces to serve.

INGREDIENT TIP: Flavor combos that are sure to please:

- Dried apricots, raisins, and almond slices
- Banana chips and peanuts
- Dried blueberries, dried strawberries, and chopped pistachios
- Dried cranberries and pecan halves topped with a little orange zest

Store in airtight containers or in heavy zip-top gallon-size bags in a dry and cool area for up to 4 weeks.

Peppermint Bark

PREP TIME: 5 minutes | WORKING TIME: 15 minutes | SETTING TIME: 15 minutes

YIELD: 1¾ POUNDS

Peppermint bark is a cornerstone of many holiday traditions. Maybe there's a special bowl set out on a table in the front hall, tempting all who stop by for a visit. Or it could be that peppermint bark arrives in a decorated box to a lucky list of friends and family. Or perhaps you don't think this treat should be squished into a few months a year. You're going to enjoy this refreshing treat all year long, and I applaud you.

EQUIPMENT:

- Medium glass mixing bowl
- Stir stick
- Parchment paper
- Baking sheet
- Knife

24 ounces (680 grams) white almond bark

½ cup (85 grams) crushed peppermint candy, plus ⅛ cup (21 grams)

2 to 4 drops peppermint extract

1. Break up and slowly melt the almond bark in a medium glass mixing bowl in the microwave for intervals of 20 seconds at a time, stirring briefly in between cooking. Keep doing this until all the pieces are melted. Make sure the almond bark does not get too hot, or it will burn.

2. Stir in ½ cup of crushed peppermint candy and mix in the peppermint extract.

3. Pour out onto a parchment-lined baking sheet and spread into an even thin layer. Sprinkle

the remaining ⅛ cup of peppermint candy on top. Let cool completely.

4. Cut into rectangles with a sharp knife, using repeated shallow cuts over the same line instead of deep cuts. This scoring process will give you a clean edge.

INGREDIENT TIP: For a dark chocolatey taste, use chocolate almond bark instead of the white almond bark. If you are feeling a bit adventurous, layer white bark on top of the dark bark for a beautiful and tasty bar. Just be sure to spread all the extra peppermint candy only on the top layer; otherwise, the two layers will not stick well.

Store in airtight containers or in heavy zip-top gallon-size bags in a dry and cool area for up to 4 weeks.

Tiger Stripes Bark

PREP TIME: 5 minutes | WORKING TIME: 15 minutes | SETTING TIME: 15 minutes

YIELD: 2 POUNDS

Candy should be three things above all else: yummy, attractive, and fun. Tiger Stripes Bark checks these boxes. What's more, there's a certain level of skill involved that, once mastered, gives the preparation of this recipe a certain guilty pleasure. It's true. You're going to worry that you have too much fun making this stuff. The particular joy we're talking about comes from seeing how a few lines of drizzled chocolate can transform into an elegant tiger swirl pattern. It's like magic, but the trick is getting the timing and the angle of the spatula just right. Once you figure that out, the finished result will be simply stunning.

EQUIPMENT:

- Medium glass mixing bowl
- Stir stick
- Small glass mixing bowl
- Silicone baking mat
- Piping cone
- Baking sheet
- Small offset spatula

24 ounces (680 grams) vanilla almond bark

¾ cup (190 grams) creamy peanut butter

1 ounce (28 grams) tempered dark chocolate or melted chocolate almond bark

1. Break up and slowly melt the vanilla almond bark in a medium glass mixing bowl in the microwave in 20-second intervals, stirring briefly in between cooking. Continue until all the pieces are fully melted. Make sure the almond bark does not get too hot, or it will burn.

2. Slowly heat the peanut butter in a small glass mixing bowl in the microwave in 10-second intervals until it is nearly a liquid, stirring frequently to prevent burning.

3. Combine the peanut butter with the vanilla almond bark and mix well. Spread evenly onto

a baking sheet lined with a silicone baking mat or parchment paper.

4. Using a piping cone with just a small opening, drizzle thin lines of the tempered dark chocolate or dark almond bark in the following pattern across the entire sheet:

- At an angle right to left: //////
- Side to side in horizontal lines: ====
- Top to bottom in vertical lines: |||||

5. Using a small offset spatula held at a slight angle with the tip against the silicone baking mat, move the spatula quickly in straight lines across the entire sheet in the following pattern:

- Side to side in horizontal lines: ====
- Top to bottom in vertical lines: |||||
- Side to side in horizontal lines: ====

6. Chill in the refrigerator for 5 minutes to set the tempered chocolate, or set on the counter if using chocolate almond bark for the drizzle. Once set, cut or break into 2-inch squares to serve.

Store in airtight containers or in heavy zip-top gallon-size bags in a dry and cool area for up to 4 weeks.

Cranberry-Walnut Easy Fudge

PREP TIME: 10 minutes | **WORKING TIME:** 10 minutes | **SETTING TIME:** 60 minutes

YIELD: 2¼ POUNDS

You might call this beginner's fudge. It's a no-fail version of traditional fudge, intended to avoid the disappointing grainy texture common in incorrectly made classic fudges.

The secret is in the finished crystal structure. Here, we use sweetened condensed milk for the bulk of the sugar component because these sugars do not form large sugar crystals that can give you that grainy texture. I include a small amount of butter and powdered sugar to mimic the firmer texture of a traditional fudge.

EQUIPMENT:

- Knife and cutting board
- Medium glass mixing bowl
- Stir stick
- Sifter
- Square glass casserole dish, greased

1 (14-ounce) can (396 grams) Eagle Brand sweetened condensed milk

1 tablespoon (15 grams) butter

16 ounces (454 grams) dark chocolate, finely chopped

½ cup (58 grams) powdered sugar

¾ cup (80 grams) walnuts, coarsely chopped

½ cup (75 grams) dried cranberries, chopped

1. In a medium glass mixing bowl, heat the sweetened condensed milk and butter in the microwave for 30 seconds. Add the chopped chocolate and stir well. Heat in 10-second increments until all the chocolate is fully melted, stirring well between heatings.

2. Sift in the powdered sugar and stir until smooth.

3. Mix in the walnuts and dried cranberries. Pour into a greased square glass casserole dish.

4. Chill in the refrigerator for 60 minutes, until firm. Cut into 1-inch squares to serve.

Store in an airtight container in the refrigerator for up to 2 weeks.

Mom's Fudge

PREP TIME: 5 minutes | **COOK TIME:** 20 minutes | **SETTING TIME:** 30 minutes

YIELD: 1¼ POUNDS

It's not uncommon for recipes to be passed down from mother to daughter through generations. In that sense, almost any recipe so passed down could safely be called "mom's (whatever) recipe." However, this one is not just any recipe. This fudge is a treasured family heirloom from my dad's side of the family. It's his mom's recipe, hence the name. And his mom's mom's fudge recipe. And quite possibly, his mom's mom's mom's recipe.

I think you'll agree that my great-grandmother's mother knew a lot about fudge making—or she got the recipe from someone else whose mother did.

EQUIPMENT:

- 4-quart saucepan
- Sifter
- Stir stick
- Pastry brush in a glass of water
- Candy thermometer
- Square glass casserole dish, greased
- Knife

2 cups (400 grams) sugar

2 tablespoons (19 grams) cocoa powder

Pinch salt

1 cup (238 grams) whole milk

2 tablespoons (28 grams) cold butter (cut into 4 pieces and kept in the refrigerator until ready to use)

1 teaspoon (4 grams) vanilla extract

1. In a 4-quart saucepan, sift together the sugar, cocoa powder, and salt, then mix in the milk. Be sure to use a 4-quart saucepan, as anything smaller will likely boil over during cooking.

2. Cook on medium heat, using the stir stick to stir just until mixture has no lumps. Remove the stir stick and wash down the sides of the pot with a pastry brush dripping with water. Insert a candy thermometer.

3. Continue cooking until the mixture reaches 235 to 238°F (soft-ball stage). Note that the mixture will boil up and then boil down again before it reaches the soft-ball stage. Remove from heat and let sit undisturbed for 10 to 12 minutes, or until the temperature has fallen to about 130°F. The mixture will look dark and shiny.

4. Add the cold butter and vanilla. Tilt the pot to one side and whip the mixture with a stir stick or electric hand mixer until it starts to thicken and has a matte look to it. Do not scrape the sides!

5. Pour into a serving platter or square glass casserole dish. Let cool completely undisturbed for about 30 minutes before cutting into 1-inch squares.

TECHNIQUE TIP: The fudge will turn grainy if the mixture is stirred while too hot. If this happens to you, don't worry; the fudge will still taste good. With the next batch, try adding ⅛ cup (41 grams) of glucose with the milk and allow the mixture to cool a bit longer before stirring to see if that fixes the texture problem.

Store in an airtight container in the refrigerator or freezer for up to 2 weeks.

ALMOND TRUFFLES, page 42

3

Chocolate & Truffles

NO FOOD IN THE WORLD HOLDS THE SAME ELEVATED place in my heart that chocolate does. This is why I became a Master Chocolatier. Chocolate is the queen of both sweet and savory foods. It's delicious, of course, with a depth of flavor rivaled by probably nothing else we eat or drink. Chocolate has many medical and emotional benefits as well. With so many different types and flavors on the market, one could experiment, invent, and innovate forever.

Chocolate

Cocoa beans are already shelf-stable without the addition of sugar, which means chocolate is not technically considered a confection (defined as a food preserved by sugar). Of course, we're interested in chocolate for its deliciousness—and because it's an extremely versatile medium—so we'll let the whole not-really-a-confection thing slide for this candy book.

For us, working with chocolate is a matter of controlling the growth of the cocoa butter crystals in much the same way we control sugar crystals in candy. There are quite a few elements to consider.

KEYS TO SUCCESS

- Always taste your chocolate prior to using it in a recipe! Your finished result will taste as good or as bad as the chocolate you use. If you are unhappy with the texture or taste (or both), try the recipe again with a different chocolate. Experimentation is part of the fun of cooking with chocolate, and it's hard to make a wrong choice.

- All the recipes in this book assume the use of commercially available chocolates. Craft chocolate often has less cocoa butter, so some of these recipes may not work as well for a beginner using craft chocolate, especially when tempering and making cream-based ganache.

- Work in a kitchen that is between 68°F and 72°F for dark chocolate and 68°F to 70°F for milk and white chocolates. If your kitchen is too warm, the chocolate will likely not temper correctly. If tempered in a too-warm environment, your chocolate may come out dull and grainy-looking when set. You may also notice that cocoa bloom (a light brownish white powder) will appear more quickly during storage.

- Keep water away from chocolate. Even a small amount can seize the chocolate, rendering it completely unusable. Seized chocolate can never be remelted and used for chocolate work. In fact, it is no longer considered chocolate on a chemical level, as the original chemical structures are broken. However, all is not lost. If you see your chocolate starting to seize, the only "fix" is to add a lot more water and/or cream and stir quickly. Then heat the mixture up to make hot chocolate!

- Working quickly is the key to success with chocolate. Go too slow, and it will start to thicken. If that happens, gently reheat the bowl of chocolate in the microwave for 10 seconds at a time, then stir for at least 30 seconds in between heatings. Heat only enough to make it workable again.

- Technique matters quite a bit for successful results. Follow directions exactly, especially when making a ganache. Do not substitute one chocolate type for another (i.e., dark for milk) unless the recipe specifically states that this is okay to do.

- Temper at least 1 pound of chocolate (2 pounds is best) when dipping. The larger mass will hold a more stable temperature, which makes for less frustrating work. When finished dipping, simply pour the extra chocolate onto a baking sheet lined with parchment paper, being sure to spread it thin. Let the chocolate set overnight in a cool room. Break up the chocolate and use as tempered chocolate for your next recipe.

- Do not use a thermometer to temper chocolate. It's just not practical. Every type and variety of chocolate is different, and each will require a different set of temperatures to be successful. Besides, temperature is only part of the tempering equation. You must allow enough time and control the movement of the chocolate to be successful.

Technique Spotlight
TEMPERING

Chocolate is defined as a suspension of cocoa solids and sugar (and sometimes milk powder) in cocoa butter. When it comes to tempering, the crystals formed by the cocoa butter inside chocolate are important. Cocoa butter is what gives chocolate its shine, hardness, snap, and smooth mouthfeel. Cocoa butter is a polymorph, meaning it can take different forms. Therefore, we need to carefully manipulate the crystals so they take the ideal form for the characteristics we want—shine, hardness, etc. This process is known as tempering.

All the recipes in this chapter require tempering. It's a good idea to practice tempering a few times before making a recipe. Start with just ½ pound of cocoa butter so you can really see what is going on. At first, when fully melted, cocoa butter is transparent, like clarified butter. But if you pour the melted cocoa butter onto a cold counter and mush it around with a pallet knife or spatula (what we call "table tempering"), you'll see it begin to change. As the cocoa butter cools down, it will start to hold air bubbles and its viscosity will increase (getting thicker). Keep mushing, and the color will start to lighten as it continues to thicken until it resembles whipped butter, eventually becoming solid when cooled completely.

There are many ways to temper chocolate. The best for beginners is known as the partial-melt method.

1. **Break the chocolate into small pieces,** leaving 2 or 3 larger chunks. Place the smaller pieces in a medium glass mixing bowl. Leave the larger chunks on the counter.

2. **Use a low-powered microwave (1000 watts) to melt the chocolate in 15-second increments**, stirring in between heating, even if it looks unchanged. Repeat until only half the chocolate is melted, and no more. It's easy to overheat and melt too many good crystals, so it's best to err on the side of less melting. At no time should you have all the chocolate melted, even while stirring. If that happens, the chocolate has become too hot, and you will need to add more unmelted chunks.

3. **Add the larger chunks to the bowl.** Stir until most of the chocolate has been melted and the chocolate feels cold again. Smear a bit of chocolate on the counter with the stir stick. It should set in a minute or two and become firm to the touch, with an even, matte look. Remember to keep stirring while you wait for the result. If it takes longer than two minutes to set, the chocolate has a weak or false temper. If so, keep stirring and testing until it's ready.

4. **Once you have determined that your bowl is in temper and is cool to the touch**, return it to the microwave for 5 to 10 seconds.

5. **Stir well.** Remove any remaining chunks before using the chocolate in a recipe. Place the chunks on parchment paper to set. They can be used for future batches or for snacking on while you work.

6. **When you're finished dipping**, pour out the extra chocolate onto a parchment-lined sheet pan and spread thin with an offset spatula. Let set fully in a cool location. Break into pieces and store in a cool, dry, dark place for use in your next batch.

Keep in mind that this method works for up to 1 pound. Larger quantities require 20- to 30-second intervals instead of 15 seconds.

Fancy Dipped Strawberries

PREP TIME: 10 minutes | **WORKING TIME:** 20 minutes | **SETTING TIME:** 5 minutes

YIELD: 3 POUNDS

Nothing impresses guests like decadent, beautifully dipped strawberries. It's almost weird how two simple elements can combine to make a treat that is both elegant and refreshing at the same time. This recipe uses tempered chocolate for its complex flavor, but you can substitute coating chocolate as an alternative to tempering.

EQUIPMENT:

- Paper towels
- Small glass mixing bowl
- Stir stick
- Parchment paper
- Parchment cone

Up to 3 pounds of fresh strawberries

16 ounces (454 grams) dark chocolate

1. Wash the strawberries twice and dry gently with paper towels.

2. Temper chocolate using the method on page 32.

3. Pick up a strawberry by holding it at the base of the leaves. Dip the strawberry in the chocolate, keeping the leaves and about ¼ inch of the strawberry's beautiful red color out of the chocolate.

4. Keeping hold of the strawberry, and in quick motions, repeatedly redip the bottom third of the strawberry 4 to 6 times. This action will remove the extra chocolate. Turn the strawberry upside down (point the tip to the ceiling) to eliminate any remaining drips.

5. Place them on parchment paper gently, pushing the strawberry ¼ inch forward to discourage any chocolate pooling at the base.

6. Repeat with the remaining strawberries. If the chocolate in the bowl starts to get thicker, reheat it in the microwave for 5 to 10 seconds. Stir well after heating.

7. To decorate, use a half-full small parchment cone or just 2 inches worth of chocolate in the corner of a freezer zip-top bag. As thin lines are considered to be more elegant than thick ones, cut the parchment cone so that it has just a tiny opening (the size of a pinhead). Starting about 1.5 inches away, drizzle chocolate across the strawberry and keep piping until you are about 1.5 inches away on the other side before changing directions. Pipe 3 or 4 lines only.

8. Let the chocolate set before serving. If your event is more than an hour away, cover the strawberries loosely with a dry paper towel and store in the refrigerator for up to 2 days. Let the strawberries come to room temperature before removing the paper towel.

Store in the refrigerator for only a day or two. Strawberries taste best on the day they are washed and dipped.

TECHNIQUE TIP: Ready for a more advanced technique? Make tuxedo strawberries by dipping the strawberries in white chocolate first. After the chocolate has set, dip the strawberries in tempered dark chocolate, but this time at an angle to cover just one side of the strawberry instead of straight down. Repeat on the other side of the strawberry to make a "V shape" for the jacket. Add a bow tie and buttons using the end of a toothpick dipped in dark chocolate.

Cashew Clusters

PREP TIME: 5 minutes | **WORKING TIME:** 20 minutes | **SETTING TIME:** 10 minutes

YIELD: 1¼ POUNDS

This is another classic in the salty-sweet category. These little beauties have such a short list of ingredients, you'll be scratching your head. How can so few things combine to create a treat so very delicious? And the recipe is easily scalable, so you can bring them to an event of any size and enjoy instant MVP status.

EQUIPMENT:

- Medium glass mixing bowl
- Stir stick
- 2 spoons
- Silicone baking mat

8 ounces (228 grams) dark chocolate

2½ cups (340 grams) salted cashews

1 teaspoon (6 grams) sea salt

1. Temper the chocolate using the method on page 32.

2. Add the cashews and stir well.

3. Use two spoons to form and scoop out teaspoon-size clumps, place them on the silicone baking mat, and lightly sprinkle the sea salt on top after every 4 or 5 clusters (before the chocolate starts to set).

4. Let set fully on the counter for at least 5 minutes before serving.

INGREDIENT TIP: Another favorite version of mine is salted peanuts in milk chocolate.

Store in an airtight container in a cool, dark place, away from scent and heat, for up to 2 weeks.

Chocolate Mendiants

PREP TIME: 5 minutes | **COOK TIME:** 10 minutes
WORKING TIME: 30 minutes | **SETTING TIME:** 5 minutes

YIELD: 1¼ POUNDS

Made popular in France, mendiants are small, thin chocolate rounds topped with dried or candied fruits and sometimes mixed nuts or seeds. The type of fruit on top represents one of four French monastic orders. The color of the fruit topping represents the color of the robes worn by one of the four orders of monks, who had taken vows of poverty. While popular today year-round, these were traditionally handed out at Christmastime in France.

EQUIPMENT:

- 2 small glass mixing bowls
- Stir stick
- Slotted spoon
- 2 silicone baking mats or parchment paper
- Baking sheet
- Wire rack
- Parchment cone

½ **cup (164 grams) glucose**

½ **cup (70 grams) chopped hazelnuts or almonds**

½ **cup (60 grams) chopped pistachios**

8 **ounces (228 grams) dark chocolate**

⅓ **cup (65 grams) chopped dried apricots**

½ **cup (56 grams) chopped dried tart cherries**

2 **teaspoons (12 grams) sea salt**

1. Preheat the oven to 350°F. Heat the glucose in a small glass mixing bowl in the microwave for 90 seconds.

2. Add the hazelnuts and pistachios and stir to fully coat the nuts with glucose. Use a slotted spoon to scoop out the nuts, letting the excess glucose drain. Place the nuts on a baking sheet lined with a silicone baking mat or parchment paper. Spread the nuts out in an even layer and bake at 350°F for about

CONTINUED»

Chocolate Mendiants CONTINUED

TECHNIQUE TIP: If the chocolate in the bowl starts to get thicker, reheat the bowl in microwave for 5 seconds. Stir well prior to filling another piping cone.

10 minutes to caramelize the sugar coating and toast the nuts. Watch to make sure they don't burn.

3. Cool fully on a wire rack and break up into small pieces once set.

4. Temper the chocolate using the method on page 32.

5. Using a parchment cone or the corner of a freezer zip-top bag filled halfway with tempered chocolate, pipe 6 to 8 small circles of chocolate (about 1 to 1.5 inches in diameter) on a clean silicone baking mat.

6. Quickly top with chopped apricots, cherries, caramelized hazelnuts and pistachios, and a light sprinkling of sea salt. Gently push the toppings into the chocolate if needed.

7. Repeat with the remaining chocolate and toppings. Never pipe more than 6 to 8 circles at once, as the chocolate will likely set partially before you can get the toppings on. Working quickly will help the process go smoothly.

INGREDIENT TIP: Mix up the toppings by combining your own favorite dried or candied fruits, nuts, and seeds.

Store in an airtight container in a cool, dark place, away from scent and heat, for up to 1 week.

Orange Truffles

PREP TIME: 5 minutes | WORKING TIME: 45 minutes | SETTING TIME: 20 minutes

YIELD: 1½ POUNDS

This simple dark chocolate, cream-based ganache will make you fall in love with chocolate all over again. You'll be amazed that chopped chocolate and hot cream can transform into a silky, smooth, pudding-like texture. It's so beautiful and full of rich flavors, it could become your favorite thing to do in the kitchen.

EQUIPMENT:

- Serrated knife and cutting board or food processor
- Medium glass mixing bowl
- 16-ounce glass measuring cup
- Stir stick
- Microplane zester
- Parchment paper
- Gloves
- Spoon
- Shallow bowl or plate

16 ounces (454 grams) dark chocolate

1 cup (230 grams) heavy whipping cream

1 orange

1 cup (80 grams) cocoa powder

1. Chop the chocolate by hand (a bread knife works best for this) or in a food processor. A uniform size is necessary. Aim for a size that is smaller than a pea but larger than powder. Be sure not to melt the chocolate. Once the chocolate is chopped, transfer it to a medium glass mixing bowl. Heat in a microwave for 30 seconds on low power to warm up the bowl and to slightly soften the chocolate.

2. In a 16-ounce glass measuring cup, carefully bring the cream just to a boil in the microwave. When the cream starts to boil, it will quickly climb up the sides, so check every 15 seconds or so after the first minute. Quickly but carefully pour the hot cream over the chocolate all at once. Using a stir stick, submerge any chocolate mounds into the cream.

CONTINUED»

Wait a full minute for the chocolate to begin melting before starting your next step.

3. Create an emulsion by stirring only in the center of the bowl with your stir stick in small but quick circles, until the ganache looks shiny and dark. As the emulsion forms, you can gradually stir in larger and larger circles until the whole bowl is combined. This whole process should take no more than 2 minutes.

4. The ganache may still have a few chunks of solid chocolate in it. These can be carefully melted by heating in the microwave for no more than 8 seconds at a time. Stir for at least 1 minute before heating again if necessary. Be careful not to overheat the ganache. This could cause the emulsion to break and the fat to separate, thus ruining the truffles.

5. Zest the orange over the bowl so as to capture as much of the orange oil as possible. Be sure not to zest too deep, as the pith (the white spongy tissue just under the colored part of the peel) can be very bitter. Stir in the zest.

6. Fill a parchment cone halfway with ganache and cut a ¼-inch opening at the bottom of the cone. Pipe the ganache in small Hershey Kiss-size mounds onto parchment paper.

Allow to set, in the refrigerator if necessary, for 10 minutes.

7. Wearing gloves, quickly squish the mounds into a rough ball shape and let rest on parchment paper. Spend no more than 2 to 3 seconds on each truffle, or it may melt too much with the heat of your hands. If your hands are hot, use double gloves and work even faster. Once all the truffles have been roughly shaped into a ball, roll each one quickly between your palms to make rounder truffles. Using a spoon, coat the truffles (no more than 3 or 4 at a time) by rolling in a shallow bowl or plate of cocoa powder.

INGREDIENT TIP: For a longer shelf life, skip the cocoa powder and dip the truffles in tempered chocolate instead. These enrobed truffles do not need to be refrigerated and will last up to 1 week. Store in a cool, dry, dark, and scent-free location.

Store in an airtight container in the refrigerator for up to 3 days.

Almond Truffles

PREP TIME: 5 minutes | **WORKING TIME:** 45 minutes | **SETTING TIME:** 20 minutes

YIELD: 3 POUNDS

These truffles are a scrumptious pick-me-up you can make with and/or for family and friends any day of the week. This recipe uses amaretto liqueur, but it can easily be made without the alcohol if that's more your style.

EQUIPMENT:

- Knife or food processor
- Shallow bowl or plate
- 2 small glass mixing bowls
- Stir stick
- Parchment paper
- Parchment cone
- 2 pairs of gloves
- Spoon

3 cups (410 grams) roasted almonds

32 ounces (908 grams) milk chocolate, divided

1 cup (227 grams) butter

60 grams amaretto liqueur

1 or 2 pinches salt

1. Use a knife, or process in the food processor on pulse, to reduce the nut pieces to slightly larger than bread crumbs (no larger than a quarter of a pea). Place in a shallow bowl or plate.

2. Temper half (16 ounces/454 grams) of the milk chocolate using the method on page 32.

3. Place the butter on parchment paper. Fold the parchment paper around the butter to form a "pillow." Microwave the butter pillow for 10 seconds. Knead the pillow to distribute the heat. Continue cooking in 5-second increments, being sure to knead well in between heating. Be very careful to not melt the butter. The consistency that you are looking for is similar to whipped butter.

4. Stir the butter into the tempered chocolate. Once it is fully incorporated, add the amaretto and salt to the ganache. Mix well to fully incorporate.

5. Fill a parchment cone halfway with ganache and cut a ¼-inch opening at the tip. Pipe the ganache in small Hershey Kiss-size mounds onto parchment paper. Allow to set, in the refrigerator if necessary, for 10 minutes.

6. Wearing gloves, squish the mounds into a rough ball shape quickly and let rest on parchment paper. Spend no more than 2 to 3 seconds on each truffle, or it may melt too much with the heat of your hands. If your hands are hot, use double gloves and work even faster. Once all the truffles have been roughly shaped into a ball, roll each one quickly between your palms to make rounder truffles.

7. Temper the remaining half (16 ounces /454 grams) of the milk chocolate in the second bowl using the method on page 32.

8. Wearing new gloves for steps 8 and 9, place up to 3 truffles in the bowl of chocolate. Working quickly, use one hand to make sure the truffle is fully coated with chocolate, then use the same hand to lift the truffle out of the bowl, allowing excess chocolate to drip away before placing in the shallow bowl or plate of prepared nuts.

9. With the other hand, use a spoon to roll each truffle in the nuts until well coated. Remove the coated truffles with the same hand and place them on parchment paper. Repeat steps 8 and 9 with the remaining truffles.

Store in an airtight container in a cool, dry, dark, and scent-free area for up to 1 week.

Strawberry-Lemonade Truffles

PREP TIME: 5 minutes | **WORKING TIME:** 60 minutes | **SETTING TIME:** 20 minutes

YIELD: 1½ POUNDS

White chocolate is a perfect choice when you want to feature a bright or zippy flavor note without having to compete with the intensity of dark chocolate. This fan-favorite truffle has a refreshing lemon zing and a smooth, bright finish. It's especially popular during the summer when the berries are at the height of their growing season.

EQUIPMENT:

- Medium glass mixing bowl
- Stir stick
- Parchment paper
- Silicone 1-inch square molds
- Two-prong dipping fork

26 ounces (734 grams) white chocolate, divided

6 tablespoons (¾ stick) (85 grams) butter

1 tablespoon (6 grams) lemon zest

2 teaspoons (10 grams) lemon juice

⅓ teaspoon (1.5 grams) tartaric acid

Pinch salt

2 tablespoons (40 grams) strawberry preserves

Transfer sheets cut into 1¼-inch squares

1. Temper all the white chocolate using the method on page 32 and verify that you have a good temper by smearing a bit of chocolate (the size of a rose petal) on the counter. This should set (get firm and look matte) within 2 minutes. Set 16 ounces aside.

2. Soften the butter in the microwave and then knead it in a parchment paper pillow (see page 42) until the butter is warm (not melted) and the consistency of face cream.

3. Mix the butter into 10 ounces (280 grams) of the tempered chocolate until the mixture is well combined and looks silky.

4. Add the remaining ingredients and stir well.

5. Pipe the ganache into 1-inch square molds. Let sit on the counter or place in the refrigerator for 20 minutes to harden. They are ready for dipping when the ganache comes out of the mold cleanly.

6. Using a two-prong dipping fork, dip the truffles in the remaining 16 ounces (454 grams) of tempered white chocolate. Decorate by placing a pink-and-yellow cocoa butter transfer-sheet design on top of each truffle before dipping the next one. Let set in a cool area for 10 to 20 minutes before taking the transfer sheet off.

INGREDIENT TIP: Transfer sheets are edible art printed on acetate or vellum sheets. You can find them easily online in many different designs. The design will transfer to the finished piece as the chocolate cools and sets. Remember to place the dull/rough side of the transfer sheet against the chocolate, or the design won't transfer onto the truffle.

TECHNIQUE TIP: If your fork is damaging to the ganache square, then cover just one side (top or bottom) with tempered chocolate first. Repeat this for all the truffles. When all are done, the chocolate on the first ones will have hardened completely. Simply turn over and dip normally. This hard bottom will prevent your truffle center from getting damaged by the fork when dipping.

Store up to 3 weeks at room temperature in a dark place away from scent and heat.

HONEY CARAMELS, page 50

Caramels & Butterscotch

MY CARAMELS HAVE WON THREE WORLD GOLDS from the International Chocolate Awards (a prestigious chocolate competition held in Europe each year) along with many other domestic and international awards. Because of these awards, I am rumored to know a thing or two about this delightful confection!

Caramels & Butterscotch

These soft, chewy, golden-colored delicacies are packed with a surprising number of complex flavors even though they are made with just a few simple ingredients: cream, butter, sugar, and usually vanilla. Caramels get their name from the amber or gold color you see when sugar is caramelized.

Caramelization is the process of heating sugar until it releases its water and starts to break down. This causes the sugar to turn from a clear liquid to a light honey hue. When heated further, the mixture progresses to a lovely amber gold and then to a rich mahogany brown before it smokes and burns, turning completely black. Each color has a different taste profile quite distinct from the others. If you have not experienced these flavor differences yet, caramelize some sugar right away and taste your way through the colors!

If caramelization isn't amazing enough, it gets even better when an amino acid comes along for the ride. A Maillard reaction happens when an amino acid is present with the caramelizing sugar. Such is the case when browning meat, baking bread, and yes, making caramels. The Maillard reaction is why those foods smell so good when cooking. In caramels, the amino acid comes from the milk, cream, or butter cooked with the sugar. The Maillard reaction brings out more complex flavors and aromas than you get with just caramelization alone. It's one of the big reasons caramels have such a heavenly toasted flavor. When done right, the taste is out of this world.

Butterscotch is another longtime favorite that's very similar to caramel. What makes it different is that butterscotch is typically made with a mixture of butter and brown sugar instead of sucrose (white table sugar). It's also cooked to a higher temperature, which makes it hard instead of soft and chewy like a caramel. The brown sugar gives butterscotch a more intense taste and a darker reddish-gold color.

One important thing to remember when making these delicious golden sweets is that you must tightly control the crystal growth or you'll end up with a lumpy mess on your hands. Unfortunately, if you're a beginning candy maker, this will happen to you at some point. It's just a part of the deal. Try not to let it get you down. To stay on the right path, use these time-honored tricks to prevent those pesky crystals from forming when you don't want them to.

KEYS TO SUCCESS

- Wash down the sides of the pot with a pastry brush dipped in water (see the technique spotlight on page 54) to remove any rogue sugar crystals.

- After the mixture boils, do not stir again until the butter is added.

- Pay attention to recipes that use corn syrup or honey. These are invert sugars that help prevent the growth of crystals.

- Adding a little bit of acid, such as lemon juice or vinegar, breaks down sucrose molecules and is another way to prevent crystal growth. Just a few drops will do the trick.

Honey Caramels

PREP TIME: 5 minutes | **COOK TIME:** 60 minutes | **SETTING TIME:** 8 to 12 hours

YIELD: 3½ POUNDS

Caramels are great on their own. But adding honey to the mix kicks their already remarkably complex, nuanced flavor up several notches into the realm of world-class perfection. However, good things simply can't be rushed, so make these the night before you plan to you serve them. It's important to leave the caramels set undisturbed for a minimum of 8 hours. This gives the crystal structure time to form as tiny as possible, helping you avoid the grainy texture that comes with larger crystals. Trust me, as hard as it may seem, the extra wait time is worth it!

EQUIPMENT:

- Oversized bowl (or sink) of ice water
- Heavy-bottomed 4-quart saucepan
- High-heat stir stick
- Pastry brush in a glass of water
- Candy thermometer
- Kitchen towel
- Silicone molds (¾-inch square cavities work best) or a 9-by-9-inch glass casserole dish (greased with butter)

½ cup (120 grams) water

1⅓ cups (480 grams) corn syrup

⅓ cup (140 grams) honey

2⅛ cups (425 grams) sugar

2 pinches sea salt

½ cup (110 grams) butter

2 cups (464 grams) heavy whipping cream

1 (14-ounce) can (396 grams) Eagle Brand sweetened condensed milk

2 teaspoons (8 grams) vanilla extract

1. Prefill an oversized bowl or sink with ice water.

2. In a heavy-bottomed 4-quart saucepan, combine the water, corn syrup, honey, sugar, and sea salt. Heat on medium and stir in a figure 8 pattern until all the sugar is dissolved and the mixture starts to boil.

3. Remove the stir stick and wash down the sides of the pot with a pastry brush dipped in water.

Insert a candy thermometer and cook without stirring until the mixture reaches 250°F.

4. Carefully add the butter and stir until fully melted, then slowly add the cream. Caution: This will cause the mixture to bubble up quickly and give off steam. Remove the stir stick and cook until the mixture reaches 250°F again.

5. Remove from heat and dip the bottom half of the pan into the ice water for 2 to 3 seconds to stop the cooking. Slowly stir in the sweetened condensed milk. Return the pot to heat and cook while stirring in a figure 8 pattern until the mixture reaches 250°F once more. Note: You will be stirring for 10 to 15 minutes here, so get comfortable. If the thermometer is in the way, wait until there are layers of bubbles before reinserting the thermometer.

6. Remove from heat and dip the bottom half of the pan into the ice water for 2 to 3 seconds to stop the cooking. Be careful not to get water in the caramel. Set the pan on a towel on a heatproof surface.

7. Add the vanilla and stir rapidly to incorporate. Carefully pour into silicone molds or into a greased 9-by-9-inch square casserole dish. Let cool on the counter undisturbed for 8 to 12 hours before unmolding or cutting into rectangles.

GIFTING TIP: Wrap caramels in cellophane or wax paper, twisting to close at both ends. Place a few wrapped caramels in small bags adorned with ribbon for gifts or party favors.

Store for 4 to 6 weeks in a dry place.

Espresso Caramels

PREP TIME: 5 minutes | **COOK TIME:** 60 minutes | **SETTING TIME:** 8 to 12 hours

YIELD: 3½ POUNDS

Have you ever noticed distinctive caramel notes in fine artisan coffees? It comes from our old friend the Maillard reaction. Roasting coffee affects the amino acids and sugars found naturally in the bean in just the same way it does in caramels. It's really no wonder that fine coffee and great caramels go hand in hand.

EQUIPMENT:

- Oversized bowl (or sink) of ice water
- Heavy-bottomed 4-quart saucepan
- High-heat stir stick
- Pastry brush in a glass of water
- Candy thermometer
- Kitchen towel
- Silicon molds (¾-inch square cavities work best) or a 9-by-9-inch square glass casserole dish (greased with butter)

½ cup (120 grams) water

1⅓ cups (480 grams) corn syrup

⅓ cup (140 grams) honey

2⅛ cups (425 grams) sugar

2 pinches sea salt

8 tablespoons (1 stick) (110 grams) butter

2 cups (464 grams) heavy whipping cream

¼ cup (21 grams) espresso grounds

1 (14 ounce) can (396 grams) Eagle Brand sweetened condensed milk

4 teaspoons (16 grams) espresso liquor

1. Prefill a sink or oversized bowl with ice water.

2. In a heavy-bottomed 4-quart saucepan, combine the water, corn syrup, honey, sugar, and sea salt. Heat on medium and stir in a figure 8 pattern until all the sugar is dissolved and the mixture starts to boil.

3. Remove the stir stick and wash down the sides of the pot with a pastry brush dipped in water. Insert a candy thermometer and cook without stirring until the mixture reaches 250°F.

4. Carefully add the butter and stir until fully melted, then slowly add the cream. Caution: This will cause the mixture to bubble up quickly and give off steam. Remove the stir stick and cook until the mixture reaches 250°F again.

5. Remove from heat and dip the bottom half of the pan into the ice water for 2 to 3 seconds to stop the cooking. Stir in the espresso grounds. Slowly stir in the sweetened condensed milk. Return the pot to heat and cook while stirring in a figure 8 pattern until the mixture reaches 250°F once more. Note: You will be stirring for 10 to 15 minutes here, so get comfortable. If the thermometer is in the way, wait until there are layers of bubbles before reinserting the thermometer.

6. Remove from heat and dip the bottom half of the pan into the ice water for 2 to 3 seconds to stop the cooking. Be careful not to get water in the caramel. Set the pan on a towel on a heatproof surface.

7. Add the espresso liquor and stir rapidly to incorporate. Carefully pour into silicone molds or into a greased 9-by-9-inch square casserole dish. Let cool on the counter undisturbed for 8 to 12 hours before unmolding or cutting into rectangles.

INGREDIENT TIP: For the best texture in the finished caramel, ask your favorite coffee roaster to "Turkish grind" your beans. This is a special process that results in extra-fine, powder-like grounds.

Store caramels in cellophane or wax paper, twisting to close at both ends. They will be good for 4 to 6 weeks if kept in a dry place.

Technique Spotlight
WATER BATH

Washing down the sides of the pot with a pastry brush dipped in water is an essential step for many recipes. A pastry brush is a thick bristled brush that is used primarily for painting butter on dough, but it's quite useful in candy making because the brush can hold a lot of water in its bristles. A large glass or mason jar is perfect for this job. Fill it halfway with warm water so it won't tip over when the pastry brush is inserted. To wash down the sides (a.k.a. a water bath), simply paint all the sides of the pot with water. Make sure that the pastry brush never touches the mixture in the pot. Try to make the water "rain" down the side of the pot, melting any sugar crystals along the way. Wet the pastry brush as needed to ensure all the sides are properly washed and free of crystals. The mixture in the pot should not contain any crystals. If it does, you'll end up with a chunky or crystalline texture that will ruin the final product.

Pecan Turtles

PREP TIME: 5 minutes | **WORKING TIME:** 30 minutes | **COOK TIME:** 5 minutes

YIELD: 3 POUNDS

"Turtles, turtles, turtles!" That's what my eldest daughter would call out anytime she came home and smelled that toasted-pecan and caramel scent in the air. Turtles are famously slow-moving creatures. However, you'll find there's nothing slow-moving about these truly divine nutty, chocolatey, caramel mashups when you put them out on the table!

EQUIPMENT:

- Baking sheet
- Silicone baking mat
- Small glass mixing bowl
- Stir stick
- Parchment piping cone or spoon
- Parchment paper

4 to 5 cups (500 grams) pecan halves

12 ounces (336 grams) Honey Caramels (page 50), cut into ¾-inch squares

½ pound (227 grams) milk or dark chocolate

Sea salt, for garnish (optional)

1. Preheat the oven to 250°F.

2. Line a baking sheet with a silicone baking mat. Place the pecans on the baking mat in sets of 3 in a starburst pattern (one end of each of the 3 pecans should be touching at the center). These will be the feet and heads of the turtles. The clusters should be about half an inch apart. Be sure not to use broken or burned nuts. Typically, there will be about 150 grams of unusable nuts.

3. Place a caramel square in the center of each nut cluster. Gently press down to make sure it won't move or fall off the nuts.

4. Put the baking sheet in the oven and cook just until the caramel is soft and begins to spread,

CONTINUED»

about 5 minutes. Remove the baking sheet from the oven. Let cool fully.

5. Temper the chocolate in a small glass mixing bowl using the method on page 32. Pipe or spoon about 1 teaspoon of chocolate onto each caramel to create the turtle's shell. Don't worry about covering all the caramel. I like to leave an even ring of caramel showing along the edges for better visual appeal. Sprinkle sea salt to garnish (if using).

DECORATING TIP: While I prefer the ratio of 3 pecans per turtle, for a fun twist add 2 more to make the candy look more like its namesake.

TECHNIQUE TIP: It can be hard to temper and work with just a half-pound of chocolate. I recommend tempering at least a pound at a time (454 grams). Once you're done making the turtles, spread out the remaining chocolate on parchment paper and let it set on a cool kitchen counter. Then store and use this tempered chocolate in a future recipe.

Store up to 2 weeks in an airtight container lined with parchment paper. It's okay to stack the turtles as long as there is a layer of parchment paper underneath.

Caramel Apples

PREP TIME: 5 minutes | COOK TIME: 10 minutes | SETTING TIME: 20 minutes

YIELD: 6 TO 8 MEDIUM APPLES

These treats were once strictly kid stuff, typically found only at county fairs and old-time jamborees. Thankfully, caramel apples have made a resurgence. Nowadays, with the right recipe, even the fanciest food critic will agree that the crisp, juicy tartness of a Granny Smith apple makes a perfect companion for the chewy, sweet, and complex flavors of fine caramel. Adults and kids can agree on that.

EQUIPMENT:

- 6 to 8 wooden apple sticks
- Small glass mixing bowl
- Pot holders
- High-heat stir stick
- Silicone baking mat or parchment paper

6 to 8 medium-size Granny Smith apples

2 pounds (908 grams) Honey Caramels (page 50)

4 teaspoons (20 grams) water

1. Remove the apple stems by twisting them off at the base. Wash the apples in warm water, being sure to remove any waxy coating. This is very important, as the caramel will not stick to the apples otherwise. Dry thoroughly.

2. Turn the apples over and stab them with the wooden stick in the center of the bottom. To get the stick so that it is three-quarters of the way into the apple without bruising or damaging the apple, turn the apple over and carefully hit the stick against the counter, but be sure to hold the apple on the sides so that your hand won't be injured by the stick if it goes too far into the apple.

3. Put the batch of Honey Caramels in a small glass mixing bowl. Add the water. Heat in a microwave for 2 minutes. Use pot holders to remove the bowl from the microwave, as the

caramel will get hot. Stir well. Repeat this process until the caramel is boiling.

4. Place the bowl on a heatproof surface. Place a silicone baking mat next to the bowl. Tilt the bowl so that the caramel is thicker on one side. Dip the apples one at a time into the caramel, leaving a small amount of color showing near the stem. Rotate the apple to coat fully. Remove the apple from the caramel with the stick straight up and down. Vigorously hit the surface of the caramel in the bowl with the apple 4 to 5 times to remove excess caramel.

5. Turn the apple upside down by the stick and spin gently to cool the caramel so that it will not simply flow off the apple when you set it down. Place the finished apples on a silicone baking mat or parchment paper. Cool fully.

TECHNIQUE TIP: By hitting the surface of the caramel in the bowl with the apple, you are using the surface tension of the caramel in the bowl to pull off excess caramel from the apple. This is due to the cohesive forces between molecules. What does this science stuff mean for us? It means that the surface of the mass in the bowl pulls the excess caramel off the apple evenly from all sides at once. Science is so cool!

Store on parchment paper squares in a cool, dry place away from light and scent for up to 1 week.

Caramel Popcorn Clusters
with Roasted Peanuts

PREP TIME: 10 minutes | **COOK TIME:** 15 minutes | **SETTING TIME:** 10 minutes

YIELD: 3 POUNDS

If you grew up eating boxes of Cracker Jack at the ballpark, you know why this caramel corn is so addictive, even without the cool prize inside each box. It has the perfect combination of salty and sweet with the crisp, light crunch of popcorn and the unmistakable texture of toasted peanuts, all rolled into one. Plus, it is easy to make for crowds of any size. Go ahead and bring a big bowl of caramel corn to your next party. It's a surefire home run.

EQUIPMENT:

- Parchment paper
- Baking sheet
- Oversized bowl
- Small prep bowl
- Heavy-bottomed 4-quart saucepan
- High-heat stir sticks
- Pastry brush in a glass of water
- Candy thermometer
- 2 silicone baking mats

2¼ cups (300 grams) roasted peanuts

3 microwave bags (200 grams) popped popcorn (about 12 cups of air-popped popcorn)

1¼ teaspoons (6 grams) baking soda

1½ teaspoons (8 grams) salt

1 cup (200 grams) sugar

¾ cup (180 grams) brown sugar

¼ cup (84 grams) maple syrup

¼ cup (90 grams) corn syrup

6 tablespoons (85 grams) butter

1. Spread the peanuts on a parchment-lined baking sheet. Warm in the oven at 200°F. Then place the popcorn in an oversized bowl next to the stove. Mix the baking soda and salt in a small prep bowl and place it next to the stove.

2. In a heavy 4-quart saucepan, stir together the sugar, brown sugar, maple syrup, corn syrup, and butter over low heat. When it looks like all the sugar crystals have melted, take out the stir stick.

3. Brush down the sides of the pot with water, using a clean pastry brush, until there are no crystals on the sides of the pot.

4. Place a candy thermometer into the saucepan and cook without stirring until the mixture reaches 290°F.

5. Remove the pan from heat and add the baking soda and salt mixture. This will cause the caramel to foam up, so be prepared for it to rise rapidly. Keep stirring until the foaming subsides a bit. Then stir in the warmed peanuts.

6. Spread the caramel-nut mixture evenly over the popcorn. Quickly toss the popcorn, using 2 high-heat stir sticks, until all the popcorn is evenly coated.

7. Pour the caramel corn onto a silicone baking mat or parchment paper. Use the stir sticks to tap the popcorn down lightly into an even layer. Let cool, then break apart into small clusters.

INGREDIENT TIP: Change it up now and then by sprinkling some smoked paprika or cayenne pepper on top of the popcorn while it cools or by using roughly chopped almonds instead of peanuts.

TECHNIQUE TIP: It is best to remove any unpopped kernels from the popcorn before using. I do this quickly by pouring all the popcorn onto the counter or into a large container and then transferring the popcorn by handfuls into the extra-large bowl. This way all the unpopped kernels are left behind, as they are heavier and will fall to the bottom of the container.

Store in airtight containers or in heavy-duty zip-top gallon-size bags in a dry, cool area for up to 3 days.

Butterscotch Suckers & Bowls

PREP TIME: 5 minutes | **COOK TIME:** 15 minutes | **SETTING TIME:** 10 minutes

YIELD: 1¼ POUNDS

If you're looking for that specially shaped decoration for a themed party or a fancy presentation for an elegant event, butterscotch has got your back. All you need is a silicone lollipop mold. They come in a mind-boggling array of shapes and sizes—everything from dancing bears and soaring spaceships to brides and grooms. There is a whole world of sucker shapes awaiting. What's more, you can use any excess to make butterscotch bowls for serving ice cream or small desserts. The possibilities are endless!

EQUIPMENT:

- Silicone lollipop molds that can withstand heat of at least 300°F
- Paper sucker sticks (plastic may melt)
- 6 to 8 small glass prep bowls
- 3-quart heavy-bottomed saucepan
- High-heat stir stick
- Pastry brush in a glass of water
- Candy thermometer
- Metal spoon
- Silicone baking mats or several sheets of parchment paper

Vegetable spray

1⅔ cups (360 grams) brown sugar, sifted to remove chunks

½ cup (180 grams) glucose

½ cup (113 grams) butter

½ teaspoon (2 grams) cream of tartar

1. Prepare lollipop molds by inserting paper sucker sticks into the slots. Set aside on a flat surface. Prepare small glass prep bowls by spraying the insides heavily with vegetable spray.

2. Combine the brown sugar, glucose, butter, and cream of tartar in a 3-quart heavy-bottomed saucepan. Stir and cook on medium heat until the sugar has dissolved and the mixture starts to boil.

3. Remove the stir stick. Wash down the sides of the pot with water and a pastry brush.

4. Insert a candy thermometer and cook without stirring until the mixture reaches 300°F (hard crack). Remove the pot from heat and let cool until the bubbling subsides a bit. A few bubbles are okay.

5. Carefully pour the butterscotch into the lollipop molds. Let it cool fully before removing from the molds.

6. With the remaining butterscotch, drizzle hot butterscotch inside the small sprayed glass prep bowls, using a metal spoon, in straight crisscrossing lines to create a thick lattice pattern or in small swirls to create a swirl pattern. Pour out any remaining butterscotch onto a silicone baking mat.

7. Remove any butterscotch that got on the outside of the bowls for a nice, clean edge. Let cool for a minute before removing the butterscotch bowls from the glass bowls using a gentle twisting motion. Let cool fully. Break up the poured disk of extra butterscotch into randomly sized pieces for use as a garnish or for snacking.

TECHNIQUE TIP: If a sucker breaks, carefully heat the edge of one of the broken pieces with a controlled flame for a second or two, just until the edge is slightly melted, then firmly hold the two pieces together for 3 or 4 seconds to "glue" them back together.

Store up to 4 weeks in a cool, dry place, or wrap suckers in cellophane sheets and close with a decorative twist tie or bow.

BUTTERCRUNCH TOFFEE, page 77

Brittle & Toffee

TOFFEE AND BRITTLE ARE OFTEN CONFUSED, AND people use their names interchangeably, but there is an important difference: only one includes butter.

Brittle

Brittles are a sugar candy made from a simple mixture of sugar and water. Sometimes they include nuts and flavorings. They are known for being on the thin side and should break and bite easily. They shouldn't be soft and chewy like caramels or so thick that you need to suck on them like lollipops.

Brittles are cooked to hard crack (300°F) and are typically somewhat transparent when cooled. In fact, a lot of "glass" in movies is actually sugar glass. Sugar glass is brittle, easy to break, and inexpensive to make and replace. It even sounds like breaking glass. Some brittle varieties use baking soda to create thousands of tiny bubbles, which expand their volume, making them easier to bite.

Toffee

Toffee is similar to brittle but with two major differences. First, it's usually quite a bit thicker than brittle, up to half an inch thick. And, second, toffee is made with a mixture of sugar and butter instead of water.

Toffee is also cooked to 300°F, though some recipes call for lower temperatures, especially when milk is added for a chewier toffee texture. But unlike brittle, you can't just walk away from the pot as toffee boils. Toffee is a diva in need of constant attention. If you stop stirring during cooking, the butter will throw a fit and separate from the sugar. But, just like in show business, a talented diva can be a showstopper. The buttery flavor and easy-shearing crystals are toffee's raw talent. Add in a costume of chocolate and nuts, and you have an unforgettable performance.

- A thin brittle must be pulled thin, so make sure you have some thick gloves to protect your hands. Be sure to pull so that even the middle gets thin, not just the sides.

- When you add baking soda to a brittle, it will expand quickly in volume. Be prepared and keep stirring!

- If you are adding nuts to your brittle, make sure the nuts are warm. Cold nuts can cause the sugar mixture to crystalize. You can add raw peanuts early. But nuts higher in fat like pecans will tend to burn, so add them toward the end.

- Making toffee requires a ton of stirring right from the beginning. Get comfortable and have a silicone baking mat ready to pour the toffee onto when done.

- While cooking, toffee will rise in the pot to more than double in size. What's more, it can "spit" streams of hot toffee without warning. A large enough saucepan is crucial, as are gloves for protection while stirring and quickly pulling the saucepan from the heat in an emergency. Long sleeves are also a good idea.

Sesame Brittle

PREP TIME: 5 minutes | COOK TIME: 30 minutes | SETTING TIME: 10 minutes

YIELD: 1½ POUNDS

These crunchy, sweet little beauties feature a nice toasted flavor without the addition of nuts. They're perfect for when you need a nut-free option or anytime you're in the mood for something a little outside the ordinary.

EQUIPMENT:

- Large skillet
- Stir stick
- Heavy-bottomed 2-quart saucepan
- Pastry brush in a glass of water
- Candy thermometer
- Silicone baking mat
- Offset spatula

1¾ cups (250 grams) sesame seeds

⅓ cup (80 grams) water

1¼ cups (250 grams) sugar

½ cup (160 grams) glucose

1 teaspoon (6 grams) sea salt

1. Toast the sesame seeds in a large skillet over medium-high heat, stirring constantly. No oil should be used. Stir for 10 to 15 minutes, until the seeds turn brown and look a bit oily. Some may even start to pop. This is good! Remove the pan from heat and set aside.

2. In a heavy-bottomed 2-quart saucepan, stir together the water, sugar, glucose, and sea salt. Stir over high heat until the mixture just starts to boil. Remove the stir stick.

3. Brush down the sides of the pot with water, using a clean pastry brush, until there are no crystals on the sides of the pot.

4. Place a candy thermometer into the saucepan and cook without stirring until the mixture reaches 310°F (hard crack).

5. Remove the pot from heat and quickly stir in the toasted sesame seeds. Pour onto a silicone baking mat and spread to an even thickness with an offset spatula. Let cool completely on the counter. Break into bite-size pieces.

TECHNIQUE TIP: If you want a specific size or shape of brittle, wait until the brittle cools just a bit, then cut it with an oiled knife into the desired size and shape. Remember to transfer the brittle to a cutting board first so you don't cut the silicone baking mat!

Store in airtight containers or in heavy-duty zip-top gallon-size bags in a dry and cool area for up to 1 week.

Cacao Origin Brittle

PREP TIME: 5 minutes   **COOK TIME:** 20 minutes   **SETTING TIME:** 20 minutes

YIELD: 2 POUNDS

Chocolate is a combination of sugar and cacao. But here we split those components apart and recombine them in a new way that releases a surprisingly nuanced flavor. We're able to get a little more depth from the sugar and play around with the bitterness of cacao and the tangy, sour notes of cherries. The result is nothing less than a bright festival for your palate.

EQUIPMENT:

- 2 silicone baking mats
- Baking sheet
- Heavy-bottomed 3-quart saucepan
- High-heat stir stick
- Pastry brush in a glass of water
- Candy thermometer
- Gloves

1¼ cups (150 grams) cacao nibs

1 cup (113 grams) chopped tart cherries

1 cup (236 grams) water

2½ cups (500 grams) sugar

¾ cup (24 grams) glucose

1 tablespoon (18 grams) salt

1. Set two silicone baking mats next to each other so that they make one large mat. Warm the nibs and chopped tart cherries on a baking sheet in the oven with the temperature set to 250°F. Leave in the oven until you are ready to use them in step 3.

2. In a heavy-bottomed 3-quart saucepan, combine the water, sugar, glucose, and sea salt. Heat on medium-high and stir in a figure 8 pattern until all the sugar is dissolved and the mixture starts to boil.

3. Remove the stir stick and wash down the sides of the pot with a pastry brush dipped in water. Insert a candy thermometer and cook without stirring until the mixture reaches 300°F.

Remove from heat and stir in the warmed nibs and cherries.

4. Pour the mixture out onto the silicone baking mats. Let cool until the brittle is still warm but stays together as one piece when lifted off the mat. Put on gloves and start pulling the brittle on all sides so there are just thin sheets of sugar decorated with loosely scattered nibs and cherry pieces.

5. Let cool fully before breaking up into small bite-size portions.

SERVING TIP: Warm brittle can be molded or pulled into cool shapes. Try forming it into a dome to place over your favorite dessert. You'll be able to gaze through the glass and eat it, too.

Store in an airtight container lined with parchment paper in a cool and dry place away from light and scent for up to 3 weeks.

Chunky Peanut Brittle

PREP TIME: 5 minutes | **COOK TIME:** 30 minutes | **SETTING TIME:** 20 minutes

YIELD: 2½ POUNDS

My love affair with candy began in childhood while helping my dad make peanut brittle during the holidays. I loved the rich, buttery scent filling the air while it cooked and cooled. Plus, he always needed help when it came to pulling the peanut brittle so that it was nice and thin. This meant that I could be first in line for the fresh finished brittle and even sneak a few broken pieces while I was "helping."

EQUIPMENT:

- 2 silicone baking mats
- Baking sheet
- Heavy-bottomed 3-quart saucepan
- High-heat stir stick
- Pastry brush in a glass of water
- Candy thermometer
- Gloves

5 cups (625 grams) raw unsalted Spanish peanuts

¾ cup (170 grams) water

2 cups (400 grams) sugar

½ cup (164 grams) corn syrup

1 tablespoon (18 grams) sea salt

½ teaspoon (2 grams) vanilla extract

1 tablespoon (14 grams) baking soda

1. Set two silicone baking mats next to each other so that they make one large mat. Warm the peanuts on a baking sheet in the oven with the temperature set to 250°F until ready to use in step 4.

2. In a heavy-bottomed 3-quart saucepan, combine the water, sugar, corn syrup, and sea salt. Heat on medium-high and stir in a figure 8 pattern until all the sugar is dissolved and the mixture starts to boil.

3. Remove the stir stick and wash down the sides of the pot with a pastry brush dipped in water. Insert a candy thermometer and cook without stirring until the mixture reaches 300°F. Remove from heat. Add the vanilla and stir rapidly to incorporate.

4. Stir in the baking soda. This will cause the mixture to rise rapidly in the pot. Quickly add the warm peanuts and stir well.

5. Pour the mixture out onto the silicone baking mats. Let cool until the brittle is still warm but stays together as one piece when lifted off the mat. Put on gloves and start pulling the brittle on all sides so there are just thin sheets of sugar between the nuts.

6. Let cool completely before breaking up into small bite-size pieces.

TECHNIQUE TIP: Work in small sections when pulling the brittle thin so you can control the thickness better. Work from the outside in, as the center will naturally stay warmer longer. The edges harden the quickest.

Store in an airtight container lined with parchment paper in a cool and dry place away from light and scent for up to 2 weeks.

Technique Spotlight
STIRRING

Stirring correctly is a very important part of creating the perfect candy. We often think of stirring as simply mixing things together, but it plays an even more significant role. The speed and pattern of stirring both matter. Stirring slowly will reduce the possibility of incorporating air bubbles, especially with thick recipe mixtures like when making a ganache for chocolate truffles. But be careful; stirring too slowly can allow hot mixtures to burn. Quick stirring is used when air should be incorporated, like when adding volume in making marshmallows. Stirring quickly reduces the risk of burning your mixture. However, if you stir too quickly, it can splash and burn you.

Whether you need to stir quickly or slowly, hot liquids are best stirred in a figure 8 pattern. It's most efficient and reduces the chances of burning. Be sure to incorporate any mixture that sticks to the sides every 20 to 30 strokes. Just scrape the sides quickly with the flat side of the stir stick, ideally with just one or two long strokes.

Old English Toffee

PREP TIME: 5 minutes | COOK TIME: 35 minutes | SETTING TIME: 20 minutes

YIELD: 2 POUNDS

Old English Toffee has just two ingredients: butter and sugar. Yep, you read that right. No nuts, no vanilla, and no chocolate in traditional English toffee. If you've got a toffee coated with chocolate and nuts, that's a whole different confection. This original "naked" version of classic English toffee is dedicated to the harmonious love affair between butter and sugar.

EQUIPMENT:

- Gloves
- Silicone baking mat
- Rimmed baking sheet
- Heavy-bottomed 3-quart saucepan
- High-heat stir stick
- Candy thermometer
- Offset spatula

2 cups (4 sticks) (454 grams) butter

2¼ cups (450 grams) sugar

½ cup (118 grams) water

⚠️ **CAUTION:** *This recipe does get a bit dangerous as the pot boils up, so please wear gloves and long sleeves when making toffee.*

1. Place a silicone baking mat on a rimmed baking sheet. Set aside. Melt the butter in a heavy-bottomed 3-quart saucepan over medium-high heat. Once the butter has melted, add the sugar and water. Stir quickly in a figure 8 pattern and keep stirring until the mixture reaches 300°F.

2. Remove from heat and pour the toffee out onto the silicone baking mat. Use an offset spatula to spread smoothly. Let cool fully before breaking up into small pieces.

3. Repeat the recipe after your arm takes a break. Not only is toffee easy to make, but it will also be eaten and gone in a blink of an eye!

CONTINUED»

Old English Toffee

TECHNIQUE TIP: To dress up this recipe for an elegant affair, use a ruler and a pizza cutter to make score lines in the toffee while it's still hot but no longer liquid. I like to make a diamond pattern with 1-by-1½-inch pieces. When the toffee is fully cooled, simply break along the score lines.

Store in an airtight container lined with parchment paper in a cool, dry place away from light and scent for up to 2 weeks.

Buttercrunch Toffee

PREP TIME: 5 minutes | **COOK TIME:** 15 minutes | **SETTING TIME:** 10 minutes

YIELD: 2 POUNDS

Buttercrunch toffee was created about a hundred years ago somewhere in Tacoma, Washington, just about an hour south of my kitchen. Back then, most almonds came from Spain. The word used to describe the hard nut inside an almond shell is "roca," which means "rock" in Spanish. This term inspired the famous American buttercrunch brand Almond Roca.

EQUIPMENT:

- Gloves
- Silicone baking mat
- Rimmed baking sheet
- Heavy-bottomed 3-quart saucepan
- High-heat stir stick
- Candy thermometer
- Offset spatula

1 cup (2 sticks) (227 grams) butter

1⅛ cups (225 grams) sugar

3 tablespoons (44 grams) water

½ teaspoon (2 grams) vanilla extract

16 ounces (454 grams) dark chocolate, divided

3 teaspoons (12 grams) salt, divided

2 cups (250 grams) roasted almonds, coarsely chopped, divided

⚠ CAUTION: *This recipe does get a bit dangerous as the pot boils up, so please wear gloves and long sleeves when making toffee.*

1. Place a silicone baking mat on a rimmed baking sheet. Set aside.

2. Melt the butter in a heavy 3-quart saucepan over medium-high heat. Once the butter has melted, add the sugar and water. Stir quickly in a figure 8 pattern and keep stirring until the mixture reaches 300°F.

CONTINUED»

INGREDIENT TIP: I like to just coarsely chop the almonds, as I feel that chunkier nuts make for a prettier finished toffee, plus chunky pieces are easier to press into the chocolate than smaller ones.

3. Remove from heat. Drizzle in the vanilla while keeping your head away from the pot, as the pot will steam. Mix well.

4. Pour the toffee out onto the silicone baking mat. Let cool fully.

5. Temper the chocolate using the method on page 32.

6. Sprinkle half the salt (1½ teaspoons) evenly over the toffee, then pour about half (8 ounces) of the chocolate over the toffee and spread quickly into an even layer with an offset spatula. Immediately sprinkle on half (1 cup) of the chopped almonds. Let cool in the freezer for 3 minutes.

7. Flip the slab over, trying to keep it in one piece. Repeat step 6 for the other side with the remaining salt, chocolate, and almonds. Let cool until the chocolate is fully set. Break apart to serve.

Store: Toffee is rumored to last up to 2 weeks in a cool, dry place away from light and scent, but it seems to always get eaten in just a day or two instead. For me, buttercrunch toffee is simply impossible to stay away from for much longer than that. If someone had to rate the addictiveness of each of the treats I make, buttercrunch would be at the top of the list, hands down!

Spicy Hog Toffee

PREP TIME: 5 minutes | **COOK TIME:** 45 minutes | **SETTING TIME:** 10 minutes

YIELD: 2½ POUNDS

Everything is better with bacon, especially toffee. But we're going whole hog and kicking an all-time classic up a notch with the addition of bacon and cayenne pepper. The original creators of toffee might be rolling in their graves, but what's the fun in living if you can't occasionally take a walk on the wild side?

EQUIPMENT:

- Gloves
- Silicone baking mat
- Rimmed baking sheet
- Skillet
- Heavy-bottomed 3-quart saucepan
- High-heat stir stick
- Candy thermometer
- Offset spatula

16 ounces (454 grams) thick-cut bacon

1¼ cups (170 grams) cashews, coarsely chopped

1 teaspoon (6 grams) sea salt

1½ tablespoons (8 grams) cayenne pepper

1⅓ cups (300 grams) butter

¼ cup (60 grams) water

2½ tablespoons (50 grams) maple syrup

1½ cups (300 grams) sugar

⚠ CAUTION: *This recipe does get a bit dangerous as the pot boils up, so please wear gloves and long sleeves when making toffee.*

1. Place a silicone baking mat on a rimmed baking sheet. Set aside. In a skillet, fry the bacon until it's extra crispy. Set aside. Wipe the remaining fat off of the skillet. Toss the cooked bacon, cashews, salt, and cayenne pepper in the same skillet and heat on low until warm. Keep warm over low heat, stirring occasionally.

CONTINUED»

2. Melt the butter in a heavy-bottomed 3-quart saucepan over medium-high heat. Once the butter has melted, add the water, maple syrup, and sugar. Stir quickly in a figure 8 pattern and keep stirring until the mixture reaches 300°F. Remove from heat.

3. Quickly stir in the warm bacon, cashew, salt, and cayenne pepper mixture.

4. Pour the toffee out onto the silicone baking mat. Use an offset spatula to spread smoothly. Let cool fully before breaking up into pieces.

Store in an airtight container lined with parchment paper in a cool, dry place away from light and scent for up to 1 week, or leave out on the counter as a warning for the other hogs to behave, or else!

ROCK CANDY, page 96

Lollipops & Hard Candy

FROM LEMON DROPS TO JAW BREAKERS TO LOLLI- pops and Jolly Ranchers, hard candy has so many variations in form, flavor, and presentation. The bright, translucent colors are mesmerizing; no candy shop or season is compete without them. Spring is sweeter with a roll of Life Savers, Summertime gets even hotter with cinnamon imperials, Halloween is filled with mouth-puckering sour pops, and Christmas isn't the same without classic red-and-white striped peppermint candy canes!

Lollipops & Hard Candy

Lollipops are probably the most iconic candy of all. No candy wonderland is complete without them. Just try to find a department store window display at Christmastime that doesn't feature the lollipop in some form or another. Happy children have been depicted through the ages holding lollipops, at least since 1908, when a guy named George Smith is said to have invented them.

The name "lollipop" comes from northern England circa the 17th century. It literally means "tongue slap," which is both weird and appropriate. Few other candies come in so many different shapes, colors, sizes, textures, and flavors. There exists such variety in the world of lollipops, one could easily imagine someone building a museum in their honor. Spoiler alert: It already exists in the Russian city of Ryazan, about 122 miles east of Moscow.

But when it comes down to it, what exactly are lollipops? If you think about it, when you take away the stick from a lollipop, what do you have? Well, aside from sticky fingers, you have the second-most recognizable candy of the all, the venerable hard candy.

Lollipops and clear hard candies are amorphous solids. Like in glass, the atoms in hard candy are not arranged in orderly patterns. And while making hard candy is quite simple, there is quite a bit of chemistry involved and several specific steps that must happen for the crystals to grow properly. But master the process, and the rewards are great.

There is just something magical about hard candy. Whether standing alone or in lollipop form, hard candy has a unique ability to bring back memories of childhood happiness. And no other hard candy conjures memories as intense or delicious as a lemon drop (at least in my opinion). Even though I am a Master Chocolatier and taste chocolate several times a day, I am pretty sure that I eat more hard candy than chocolate in any given week, especially my favorite candy of all time, lemon drops! They have a hard, glass-like quality, just begging you to shatter them with your teeth. And once you melt off all the yummy, tart, powdered sugar coating, you're treated to a magical lemony sweetness that conjures up all sorts of youthful happiness. I have been known to finish off an entire bag in one sitting. But that's me. You probably have your own memories, and I bet hard candies play a role in some of them. If not, let's create some, shall we?

Technique Spotlight
USING A CANDY THERMOMETER

When cooking candy, proper use of a thermometer is essential. You cannot obtain the desired firmness or texture of candies prepared with a mixture of sugar and water without careful, timely, and correct temperature measurements. The first step is to calibrate your thermometer as described on page 2. Then be sure to read the temperature of the boiling sugar by placing the thermometer one-third of the distance between the side of the pot and the center. And, of course, keep the probe from touching the bottom of the pot at all times. The closest you should get is about a quarter of an inch. Follow these guidelines, and you can be confident you're getting the average temperature of the hot liquid.

Fancy Lollies

PREP TIME: 5 minutes | **COOK TIME:** 20 minutes | **SETTING TIME:** 10 to 15 minutes

YIELD: 1¼ POUNDS

Lollipops are a super versatile candy. You can mold them into any shape or color you want. And the flavor options are infinite. The lollipop's flexibility is particularly handy when one needs raspberry-flavored rose-shaped treats to match the exact shade of magenta on the bridesmaids' dresses. Or perhaps apple-flavored green dinosaurs on a stick for a child's birthday party. With so many silicone molds and flavorings available, these fancy lollipops can be adapted to fit any theme imaginable!

EQUIPMENT:

- Baking sheet
- Parchment paper
- Silicone lolli-pop molds
- Paper lolli-pop sticks
- Heavy-bottomed 2-quart saucepan
- High-heat stir stick
- Pastry brush in a glass of water
- Candy thermometer
- Spoon

1 cup (330 grams) water

½ cup (120 grams) glucose

2 cups (400 grams) sugar

Liquid food col-oring (optional)

1 to 2 teaspoons (5 to 10 grams) candy flavoring or extract

1. Line a baking sheet with parchment paper and place lollipop molds on the parchment paper. Prepare the molds by inserting paper lollipop sticks so that each will be at least halfway into the finished lollipop. Set aside.

2. In a heavy-bottomed 2-quart saucepan, combine the water, glucose, and sugar. Heat on medium-high and stir in a figure 8 pattern until all the sugar is dissolved and the mixture starts to boil.

3. Remove the stir stick and wash down the sides of the pot with a pastry brush dipped in water. Insert a candy thermometer and cook without stirring until the mixture reaches 300°F. Remove from heat and stir in the food coloring (if using).

4. Once all or most of the bubbles have popped, stir in the desired candy flavoring or extract (1 to 2 teaspoons is ideal). Start by adding just 1 teaspoon. Taste the mixture by cooling a drop or two on the counter to see whether you need more.

5. Spoon the mixture into the lollipop molds. Reheat as necessary to keep the liquid warm enough to spoon into the molds. Let set until firm. Package the finished lollipops in clear plastic bags and tie with a ribbon high on the stick, just below the candy.

TECHNIQUE TIP: Match colors to the added flavors as an indicator. For example, cherry lollipops should be red, lemon lollipops should be yellow, and apple lollipops are best colored with a light-green color, etc.

Store up to 3 weeks in airtight containers, or package them in cellophane bags tied with a ribbon to present as gifts.

Whiskey Pops

PREP TIME: 5 minutes | **COOK TIME:** 20 minutes | **SETTING TIME:** 10 to 15 minutes

YIELD: 1¼ POUNDS

Here's one for the rough and tough cowboy in your life. It's hard to imagine a man like this sucking on a watermelon and strawberry swirl lollipop. But fear not, there's a lolly for everyone. Just like chocolate and peanut butter, whiskey and hard candy are two great tastes that taste great together. Because, after all, why should kids have all the fun?

EQUIPMENT:

- Baking sheet
- Parchment paper
- Silicone lollipop molds
- Paper lollipop sticks
- Heavy-bottomed 2-quart saucepan
- High-heat stir stick
- Pastry brush in a glass of water
- Candy thermometer
- Spoon

1 cup (330 grams) whiskey

½ cup (120 grams) glucose

2 cups (400 grams) sugar

Liquid food coloring (optional)

Extra sugar for presentation (optional)

1. Line a baking sheet with parchment paper and place lollipop molds on the parchment paper. Prepare the molds by inserting paper lollipop sticks so that each will be at least halfway into the finished lollipop. Set aside.

2. In a heavy-bottomed 2-quart saucepan, combine the whiskey, glucose, and sugar. Heat on medium-high and stir in a figure 8 pattern until all the sugar dissolves and the mixture starts to boil.

3. Remove the stir stick and wash down the sides of the pot with a pastry brush dipped in water. Insert a candy thermometer and cook without stirring until the mixture reaches 300°F. Remove from heat and stir in the food coloring (if using).

4. Pour or spoon the hot mixture into the lollipop molds. Reheat as necessary to keep the liquid warm enough to spoon into the molds. Let set until firm. Fill cocktail glasses with extra sugar (if using) and stick a couple of lollipops in each glass to display.

INGREDIENT TIP: Hard liquor works best, but this will work with just about any alcohol. Keep in mind that the added sugar can make the mixture caramelize easier and quickly turn an amber color.

Store up to 3 weeks in airtight container, or package them in cellophane bags tied with a ribbon to present as gifts.

Root Beer Balls

PREP TIME: 5 minutes | **COOK TIME:** 15 minutes | **SETTING TIME:** 20 minutes

YIELD: 1½ POUNDS

My brother Bob loved root beer barrels as a boy, so much that he would hide them away from the rest of us. Root beer is one of the all-time classic flavors. It evokes visions of soda fountains and hot summer days. It's sweet and familiar but also unique and oh so delicious in liquid form, and now, with this recipe, you can carry it around in your pocket.

EQUIPMENT:

- Silicone sphere molds
- Heavy-bottomed 2-quart saucepan
- High-heat stir stick
- Pastry brush in a glass of water
- Candy thermometer

⅓ cup (78 grams) water

3 tablespoons (45 grams) glucose

½ cup (100 grams) sugar

1 teaspoon (5 grams) root beer flavoring or concentrate

1. Prep molds by placing the two halves of a silicone sphere mold firmly together. Set aside.

2. In a heavy-bottomed 2-quart saucepan, combine the water, glucose, and sugar. Heat on medium-high and stir in a figure 8 pattern until all the sugar is dissolved and the mixture starts to boil.

3. Remove the stir stick and wash down the sides of the pot with a pastry brush dipped in water. Insert a candy thermometer and cook until the mixture reaches 300°F. Remove from heat.

4. Stir in the root beer flavoring. Pour the mixture into the silicone molds. Cool fully on the counter for 20 minutes or until firm. Remove from the molds.

GIFTING TIP: These look super cool presented in a mason jar. Screw on a lid, and you have an airtight container that doubles as a gift. The recipient can enjoy them as is, or maybe try using them in a game of candy marbles on low-humidity days.

Store up to 3 weeks in airtight containers.

Lemon Drops

PREP TIME: 5 minutes | **COOK TIME:** 15 minutes | **SETTING TIME:** 60 minutes

YIELD: 1½ POUNDS

Irresistibly sweet and tangy, and dusted with mouth-puckering tartness, lemon drops are the king of hard candies for me. They used to be sold as cough suppressants or remedies for a dry mouth, which sort of makes sense. They're a slightly grown-up sort of candy. Fun fact: They're called drops because confectioners used to separate the long strips of candies their machines produced by, you guessed it, dropping them on hard counters. Nowadays, we just use silicone molds. Three cheers for progress.

EQUIPMENT:

- Heavy-bottomed 1.5-quart saucepan
- Stir stick
- Pastry brush in a glass of water
- Candy thermometer
- Silicone drop molds or silicone baking mat

¾ cup (150 grams) warm water

3¼ cups (650 grams) sugar, divided

Pinch tartaric acid

Pinch citric acid

5 drops (1 gram) lemon oil

3 drops yellow food coloring

1. Place the warm water and 3 cups of sugar (in that order) into a 1.5-quart heavy-bottomed saucepan. Heat on high. Stir to dissolve the sugar completely. Continue stirring until the liquid begins boiling.

2. Remove stir stick. Brush sides of the pot with water, using a clean pastry brush, until there are no crystals on sides of the pot.

3. Place a candy thermometer into the saucepan and cook without stirring until the mixture reaches 310°F (hard crack). If the liquid starts to turn yellowish/orange, it got too hot and will have a bitter taste.

4. Remove the pan from heat and allow the mixture to stop bubbling. Stir in the tartaric acid, citric acid, lemon oil, and food coloring.

CONTINUED»

TECHNIQUE TIP: If you are not using a silicone drop mold, an alternative method is to pour the mixture onto a silicone baking mat instead. While the liquid is hot but not runny, use the silicone baking mat to fold the mixture in half onto itself (like an omelet). Quickly repeat the folding action 20 or so times to create air pockets for candies that are easier to bite. Cut into small pieces while still warm, then toss with sugar to coat.

5. Pour into the silicone molds. Cool on the counter.

6. Toss the pieces with the remaining sugar to coat.

INGREDIENT TIP: For smaller coating sugar crystals, pulse the sugar in a blender for 10 seconds. For a sour punch, add 1 gram of tartaric acid to the sugar before pulsing in a blender.

Airtight containers are best for storing the drops, but I often store them in small paper bags and have never had any issues as long as it's not too humid.

Icicle Chips

PREP TIME: 5 minutes | **COOK TIME:** 5 minutes | **SETTING TIME:** 12 to 24 hours

YIELD: ⅛ POUND

Winter is one of my favorite seasons for two reasons. The cool, refreshing, crisp air and the mesmerizing shimmer of the icicles that form on the roofline of my front porch. This recipe is my way of enjoying a little piece of winter magic all year-round. Plus, these icicle chips have the added benefit of being sugar-free and xylitol-free.

EQUIPMENT:

- Rimmed baking sheet
- Silicone baking mat
- 2-cup glass measuring cup
- Stir stick

1 cup (200 grams) isomalt, precooked

Pinch citric acid

3 to 5 drops flavoring of choice

1. Line a rimmed baking sheet with a silicone baking mat. Set aside.

2. Place the isomalt and citric acid into a 2-cup glass measuring cup. Cook in the microwave in 30-second intervals until fully melted.

3. Remove from the microwave and stir in the flavoring of choice. Pour onto the silicone baking mat. Let cool and dry fully on the counter for 12 to 24 hours before breaking into small pieces.

INGREDIENT TIP: Isomalt is a manmade sugar substitute used to make sugar-free candies. You can find it online in just about any color you want. Search for "ready-to-use isomalt" or "isomalt nibs" but stay away from "isomalt crystals," as they're a bit more difficult to use.

Store in a dry tin or container that is easy to open for repeat snacking.

Rock Candy

PREP TIME: 5 minutes | **COOK TIME:** 10 minutes | **SETTING TIME:** 3 to 14 days

YIELD: 3 TO 6 STICKS

Rock candy reminds my husband of visiting crystal caves as a child. He loved looking at geodes with their colorful crystal formations. Most kids do. If you don't have geodes on hand, or for that matter, a crystal cave, growing rock candy can be just as much fun. Nothing beats rock candy as a science project. It demonstrates a lot about crystals and sugar solutions. It's messy and sticky, key attributes for holding kids' attention. But best of all, as science experiments go, it may be the most delicious of all.

EQUIPMENT:

- 3 to 6 long wooden skewers
- 3 to 6 small Mason jars, or other tall cylindrical glasses
- Heavy-bottomed 3-quart saucepan
- Stir stick
- 6 to 12 clothespins (or 3 to 6 cardboard squares)

3¼ cups (650 grams) sugar, divided

Liquid food coloring (optional)

1 cup (236 grams) water

1. Prepare wooden skewers by wetting the bottom half of the skewers and rolling them in ¼ cup of sugar to coat. Tap off excess sugar. Leave to dry at least 10 minutes.

2. Prepare glass jars by rinsing with hot water. Add 1 drop of liquid food coloring (if using) to each jar. Set aside.

3. In a heavy-bottomed 3-quart saucepan, bring the water to a boil. Stir in 1½ cups of the sugar until dissolved and heat until the water is boiling again.

4. Stir in the another 1½ cups of sugar and stir until the sugar is fully dissolved. Remove from heat. Let the mixture cool for 20 minutes.

5. Pour the sugar mixture into the jars. Place a wooden skewer in each jar, making sure that the skewer is about 1 inch from the bottom.

Secure each skewer with 2 clothespins (situated so that they are attached to the skewers in opposite directions to span the width of the glass). Alternatively, you can use cardboard squares with a small hole in the center that will hold the skewer tightly in place.

6. Set on the counter and leave undisturbed for 3 to 14 days. The longer you leave them, the bigger the rock candy will be. When ready to remove from the jar, tap the top of the liquid to crack the surface. Remove the rock candy. Dump out the remaining contents of the jar. Rehang in empty jars to dry.

EQUIPMENT TIP: Using mason jars takes a lot of sugar syrup. If you want to use less sugar syrup or make more rock candy sticks with the same amount of syrup, use a tall cylindrical glass instead. Champagne flutes work great for this. Just remember that they can tip over and break easily!

Storing in just about any container will work. As long as they stay dry, these rock candy sticks will be good for weeks and weeks.

MICROWAVE CHAMPAGNE GUMMY BEARS, page 102

Gummies & Chews

NOTHING BRINGS OUT THE KID INSIDE ALL OF US LIKE gummies and chews. These soft yet firm flavor-packed wiggly candies can be pulled and tugged in every direction before they snap back into place again and again. Go ahead. Play with your food. I'll allow it . . . and will join you!

Gummies & Chews

Kids love teddy bears. And kids love squishy candy. When German candy maker Hans Riegel put those two elements together, he created an instant candy sensation. In fact, his new candy set off a gummy craze all across Germany in the mid-1920s. Those little bears are still the most popular shape of gummy candy in the world. It's been said nearly half of all the world's gelatin goes into making gummy candies.

Soft candy is often made from pectin, as well. It can be hard to know the difference between gelatin and pectin when starting out. But don't worry, it is not too complicated.

Anything made with gelatin will have a stretchy feel when squished or pulled. And when you let go, it bounces back and wiggles like a happy dog getting a tummy rub. While gelatin is super simple to use, there are a couple downsides. It can melt in warm environments, and it is not vegan-friendly because gelatin is made from a protein derived from connective tissues harvested from animals. When allowed to absorb water and rehydrate, it will "bloom" and expand. This is best done in cold water, as heat at this stage can weaken or destroy the gelatin's gelling ability. Unlike most candies, where the sky's the limit in terms of available flavor options, there are a few fruits that just don't work with gelatin. These fruits contain an enzyme that will prevent the gelatin from getting firm. These include mango, guava, papaya, pineapple, kiwi, ginger root, and figs.

Pectin is used for making even softer candy where the flavor is of primary importance, such as Pâte de Fruit. Pectin has a couple big advantages over gelatin. Pectin doesn't melt in hot weather, and it's vegan-friendly. That said, pectin can be notoriously difficult to work with. Different brands can behave in vastly different ways. For that reason, I only included a single recipe calling for pectin (Pâte de Fruit, page 110). Make sure you use the exact brand and type of pectin indicated in the recipe (it is readily available online). Despite the pitfalls and potential frustration, Pâte de Fruit is well worth the effort.

Technique Spotlight
FILLING MOLDS

Gelatin candies are quick to make and super tasty, but they set very quickly, which can be a source of frustration for the beginner candy maker. Quickly pouring the hot liquid into the molds with a steady hand is key to success here. If you run into trouble, try using a spoon or even a turkey baster to fill the mold. Resist the urge to scrape the top of the mold to remove excess liquid. You'll end up spreading a thin layer of candy, resulting in a gummy web linking all of your pieces together. It's better to make smaller batches using larger molds until you get the hang of working faster.

Microwave Champagne Gummy Bears

PREP TIME: 5 minutes | **COOK TIME:** 5 minutes | **SETTING TIME:** 15 minutes

YIELD: ½ POUND

Fresh gummy bears are nothing like the ones you get in stores. Once you taste them, you'll never go back. Your friends will start calling you a snob, saying you're too fancy for store-bought gummies. At this point, you have a choice. You either go back to stale, old-tasting gummies—or you double down with a sparkling bowl of fresh Champagne gummy bears.

EQUIPMENT:

- Mini gummy bear silicone molds
- Baking sheets
- 4-cup glass measuring cup
- Stir stick
- Spoon

⅔ **cup (156 grams) Champagne (or sparkling rosé)**

¼ **cup (50 grams) sugar**

4 packets (28 grams) gelatin

1. Put silicone mini gummy bear molds on baking sheets. Set aside.

2. In a 4-cup glass measuring cup, combine the Champagne and sugar. Gently sprinkle a third of the gelatin on top of the Champagne mixture. Wait for the gelatin to bloom (about 1 minute), then poke it down with the stir stick. Sprinkle another third of the gelatin and wait for it to bloom. Repeat for the last third. Gently stir to incorporate well and to bloom all the gelatin.

3. Microwave for 30-second increments, stirring briskly in between heating. Continue until all the sugar and gelatin have dissolved. The

mixture will foam up. This is okay just as long as it does not spill over.

4. Once the sugar and gelatin have dissolved, use a spoon to skim off the layer of foam. This will make your gummies clear and sparkly!

5. Pour the mixture into the gummy bear silicone molds. Cool in freezer for 15 minutes or until firm. Remove the gummy bears from the molds.

TECHNIQUE TIP: This recipe is easy to double, but I don't recommend it. You may not be finished pouring before the gelatin starts to thicken. It is best to make several smaller batches instead.

GIFTING TIP: Fill small airtight containers like mini mason jars with these to serve at weddings.

Store in airtight containers in the refrigerator for up to 1 week.

Sour Gummy Worms

PREP TIME: 5 minutes | **COOK TIME:** 15 minutes | **SETTING TIME:** 20 minutes

YIELD: 1 POUND

Summertime is a perfect time to eat worms. Especially if those worms are artfully displayed atop a layer of crushed Oreo cookie "dirt" covered with a cheek-puckering sour dusting of sugar. It also helps if those worms are made out of fresh sour gummy candy. Unless you are a bird, gummy worms are so much tastier, and they have the added bonus of being easier to keep from squirming off the display.

EQUIPMENT:

- Silicone gummy worm molds (if using)
- Rimmed baking sheets
- Parchment paper
- Gallon-size zip-top bag
- Medium glass mixing bowl
- Stir stick
- Heavy-bottomed 2-quart saucepan
- Knife or cookie cutter (if not using molds)

⅛ **cup (25 grams) tartaric acid**

1⅓ **cups (312 grams) apple juice**

8 packets (56 grams) gelatin

½ **cup (100 grams) sugar**

Food coloring (optional)

1. Place silicone worm molds on the rimmed baking sheets if using, or line the baking sheets with parchment paper. Place the tartaric acid in a gallon-size zip-top bag. Set aside.

2. Pour the apple juice into a medium glass bowl. Sprinkle half of the gelatin over the juice. Wait 1 minute for the gelatin to bloom. Poke down with a stir stick. Repeat the process with the second half of the gelatin. Gently mix to incorporate fully. Let sit for 3 minutes and stir gently to break up any large chunks.

3. Pour the gelatin and juice mixture into a heavy-bottomed 2-quart saucepan. Stir in the sugar. Heat on medium while stirring in a

figure 8 pattern to make sure all the gelatin is dissolved. Bring the mixture to a boil. Add a couple of drops of food coloring (if using). Remove from heat.

4. Pour into the silicone worm molds or pour onto the parchment paper–lined baking sheets with sides and spread out to the desired thickness. Place in the freezer for 20 minutes or until firm.

5. Remove the worms from the mold and shake in the zip-top bag containing the tartaric acid. If not using a mold, simply cut thin strips and then shake in the zip-top bag containing the tartaric acid.

Store in the refrigerator in an airtight container for up to 1 week.

Gummy Soda Bottles

PREP TIME: 10 minutes | **COOK TIME:** 5 minutes | **SETTING TIME:** 60 minutes

YIELD: ONE 20-OUNCE BOTTLE OR FORTY ½-OUNCE GUMMIES

My husband and boys cannot resist picking up a pack of soda bottles whenever they find them at the store. One of the great pleasures of candy making can be transforming a favorite flavor into a new form. My favorite way to make soda bottles is to make one life-sized gummy soda bottle that will fool everyone who sees it. It is so cool when a food can steal the show at a party!

EQUIPMENT:

- Silicone soda bottle molds or plastic soda bottle*
- Baking sheets
- Medium glass mixing bowl
- Stir stick
- Heavy-bottomed 3-quart saucepan
- Parchment paper

1 (20-ounce) plastic bottle of Sprite (or Dr. Pepper)

10 packets (70 grams) gelatin

6 ounces (170 grams) lime Jell-O (or cherry Jell-O when using Dr. Pepper soda)

1. Place silicone soda bottle molds on baking sheets.

2. Pour the soda into a medium glass mixing bowl. Leave on the counter for 10 minutes to reduce the amount of carbonation (make flat). Rinse out the plastic soda bottle.

3. Sprinkle half of the gelatin over the soda. Wait 1 minute for the gelatin to bloom. Poke down with a stir stick. Repeat the process with the second half of the gelatin. Gently mix to incorporate fully. Let sit for 3 minutes and stir gently to break up any large chunks.

4. Pour the gelatin and soda mixture into a heavy-bottomed 3-quart saucepan. Heat on medium while stirring in a figure 8 pattern to make sure all the gelatin is dissolved. Bring the mixture to a boil. Remove from heat.

5. Add the Jell-O and stir until it's fully dissolved.

6. Pour into the silicone soda bottle molds, or if you're really crafty, pour it back into the plastic soda bottle.* Place in the freezer for 20 minutes or until firm. Remove from the mold and place on parchment paper.

*PLASTIC SODA BOTTLE INSTRUCTIONS:

Start with step 2 of the instructions. Then prep the plastic bottle by slitting the back of the label with a sharp knife, then peel off the label, keeping it in one piece. Save the label for use later. Then cut a 1½- to 2-inch slit lengthwise (top to bottom) where the label was and cover it with a couple of pieces of duct tape so that no liquid can come out. Remove the cap and pour in the gelatin mixture. Set in the freezer for 1 hour. Remove the duct tape. Using a sharp knife or X-Acto blade, start at the pre-made slit and carefully cut away the plastic bottle, ideally so the top and bottom sections can be pulled off the finished gummy soda bottle in as few pieces as possible. Once the plastic is fully removed, reattach the label to the gummy soda bottle (it will stick by itself) and place the plastic cap on the gummy soda bottle for a finished gummy soda bottle that will delight all your guests!

Store in an airtight container or refrigerate for up to 1 week.

Cranberry Energy Chews

PREP TIME: 5 minutes | COOK TIME: 15 minutes | SETTING TIME: 20 minutes

YIELD: 1½ POUNDS

Nothing beats Red Bull for quick energy on the go or a flavorful pick-me-up while out on the bike trail. But what about those times when drinking a whole can at once is too much? Enter Cranberry Energy Chews. With a plastic bag of these little babies along for the ride, you can be sure your get-up-and-go never up and disappears.

EQUIPMENT:

- Medium glass mixing bowl
- Heavy-bottomed 2-quart saucepan
- High-heat stir stick
- Pastry brush in a glass of water
- Candy thermometer
- Silicone molds (1-inch-diameter-by-½-inch-deep rounds work well)
- Parchment paper

1½ cups (358 grams) cold water, divided

1 (12-ounce)can (365 grams) cranberry Red Bull

8 packets (56 grams) gelatin

1 cup (200 grams) sugar

Cornstarch, for coating (optional)

1. In a medium glass mixing bowl, combine ½ cup of cold water and the cranberry Red Bull. Bloom the gelatin by sprinkling half of the gelatin over the water and Red Bull mixture. Wait for the gelatin to dissolve, about 1 minute. Poke down the bloomed gelatin with a stir stick. Repeat with the second half of the gelatin.

2. In a heavy-bottomed 2-quart saucepan, combine the remaining 1 cup of water and the sugar. Heat on medium-high, stirring in a figure 8 pattern until all the sugar is dissolved.

Remove the stir stick. Wash down the sides of the pot using a pastry brush dipped in water. Place a candy thermometer in the pot and boil the mixture without stirring until it reaches 300°F. Remove from heat.

3. Add the bloomed gelatin to the pot and stir to dissolve the gelatin. Return the pot to the stove and heat on low. Stir continuously to dissolve the gelatin fully. Remove from heat.

4. Pour the mixture into silicone molds. Cool in the freezer for 20 to 30 minutes or until firm. Remove the chews from the molds and set out on parchment paper. Leave out to dry for up to 4 hours. Coat with cornstarch (if using) to keep the pieces from sticking together.

STORAGE TIP: These are perfect for taking to sporting events in zip-top bags or other airtight containers (out of the heat, as they can melt). Just be sure to keep them away from kids, as these Cranberry Energy Chews are meant for adults only.

Store in airtight containers for up to 2 weeks in the refrigerator.

Pâte de Fruit

PREP TIME: 5 minutes | **COOK TIME:** 15 minutes | **SETTING TIME:** 2 hours

YIELD: 1 POUND

Simple, elegant, and sparkling with sugary sprinkles, Pâte de Fruit is quintessentially French. This dessert candy usually makes its appearance at the end of an elegant meal beside a warm cup of tea or coffee. I like to make a few different flavors and then place an assortment in a small box or gift bag as a memorable gift for my dinner guests to enjoy on their way home. These elegant little boxes make excellent special-occasion gifts as well.

EQUIPMENT:

- 6-inch cake pan (or square plastic container)
- Plastic wrap
- Small glass mixing bowl
- Heavy 2-quart saucepan
- Whisk
- Knife or pizza cutter

6 tablespoons (64 grams) pectin (I use Ball brand, Classic pectin)

1 cup (200 grams) sugar, divided

1 cup (260 grams) apricot-peach juice

1 tablespoon (14 grams) lemon juice

⅓ cup (67 grams) sugar, for coating (optional)

1. Prepare a cake pan by lining the bottom and sides with a large piece of plastic wrap. Set aside.

2. In a small glass mixing bowl, mix the pectin with ½ cup of sugar. Stir well.

3. In a heavy 2-quart saucepan, heat the fruit juice and lemon juice until warm (not boiling yet). Slowly whisk in the pectin and sugar mixture. Keep whisking until the mixture comes to a full rolling boil.

4. Slowly whisk in the remaining ½ cup of sugar. Continue whisking until the mixture reaches a full rolling boil again, then whisk for an additional 2 minutes.

5. Pour into the prepared cake pan. Let cool on the counter for 2 hours before removing from the pan by lifting the plastic wrap.

6. Cut into cubes with a knife or pizza cutter. Coat by rolling in sugar (if using). Leave out on the counter for 12 to 24 hours to dry fully, turning the pieces over every 4 hours.

TECHNIQUE TIP: If the finished Pâte de Fruit turns out too soft and does not hold its shape, then it likely needs to be cooked 15 to 30 seconds longer during step 4. Conversely, if it is too hard, cook it 15 to 30 seconds less.

INGREDIENT TIP: You can use just about any flavor of juice, keeping in mind that thicker or pulpy juices will work better than very thin juices.

Store on the counter for up to 2 weeks in a dry location.

PEPPERMINT PATTIES, page 120

Mints & Party Favors

LIFE IS WORTH CELEBRATING! LET'S MAKE SOME cool, refreshing treats for everyday enjoyment of little victories and some sweet memories for when its time to party in style!

Mints & Party Favors

Candy making is fun, satisfying, and delicious. However, recipes that require boiling sugar mixtures can be dangerous with small children. If you're hoping to share the experience with young kids or would rather avoid adding heat to your home during hot summer days, this chapter is for you.

Here we'll focus on recipes that require mixing and blending instead of cooking.

Marzipan has played a role in holiday traditions worldwide for over a thousand years. In southern Europe, it is commonly made into little fruit-shaped candies. People in Denmark, Sweden, and Norway enjoy eating it pig-shaped at Christmas and egg-shaped at Easter, and for the New Year, it comes as a large cake. While marzipan is traditionally made with almonds, popular variations contain peanuts, cashews, and pistachios.

Mints are most commonly used to keep our breath smelling fresh, but did you know that mints were first made popular in the 18th century by folks looking for help with their digestion? This is a cool bonus after a particularly heavy meal. Most mints, including peppermint patties and butter mints, can be made into cute party favors on a very tight budget, too. Extra cool!

Marzipan, mints, and the other treats featured in this chapter mostly rely on powdered sugar rather than standard table sugar, which has a grainier, sand-like texture. Powdered sugar is basically just table sugar that has been pulverized into a powder with just a little cornstarch added so it won't clump. It's readily available at most supermarkets but can go by many different names. Be on the lookout for bags or boxes of powdered sugar with names like "confectioners' sugar," "10X sugar," or "icing sugar." In a pinch, you can make it yourself with a blender or food processor. It won't be exactly the same, but it will do the trick for most recipes.

Technique Spotlight
WORKING WITH CANDY DOUGH

Several of the recipes in this chapter require making a candy dough. Kneading candy dough is just like kneading bread dough. Start by dusting the counter with a fine sprinkling of powdered sugar so the dough doesn't stick to the counter. Fold the dough over on itself and press down with the heel of your hands, give it a half-turn, and repeat the process. This can take some effort, so consider enlisting helpers. If the dough is too sticky, work in more powdered sugar. Just be sure to add a little bit at a time; it's easy to overdo it. When properly done, the finished candy dough should look smooth and, when squished, feel supple without cracking. Just like when making bread, it's important to keep candy dough from drying out or forming a crust. Working quickly helps avoid crusting over. Also, keep any candy dough you're not actively working with wrapped in plastic and stored in the refrigerator.

Minty Breath Pebbles

PREP TIME: 5 minutes | WORKING TIME: 30 minutes | SETTING TIME: 4 to 8 hours

YIELD: ⅛ POUND (LOADS OF MINTS)

I like to go all-out while making my gingerbread house every year, complete with elaborate garden scenes all around. These adorable mint-packed pebbles are the perfect decorating candy for creating realistic rock pathways and riverbeds. Plus, they are super easy to make and great to keep on hand to pop in your mouth whenever you need an intense breath-scrubbing dose of cinnamon or peppermint on the fly.

EQUIPMENT:

- Rimmed baking sheet
- Parchment paper
- Small glass mixing bowl
- Stir stick
- Rolling pin
- Wide plastic straw (bubble-tea straw) cut down to 1 inch in length
- Wooden apple stick

1 cup (115 grams) powdered gum paste mix

2 to 3 teaspoons (10 to 15 grams) hot water, divided

5 to 10 drops extract flavoring (such as cinnamon or peppermint)

1 drop food coloring (optional)

Dusting of powdered sugar, for rolling

1. Line a rimmed baking sheet with parchment paper. Set aside.

2. Add the powdered gum paste mix to a small glass mixing bowl. Stir in 2 teaspoons hot water, the flavoring, and the food coloring (if using). Turn out onto the counter and knead by hand to form a ball.

3. Taste a small amount and add additional drops of flavoring until you reach the desired strength. Add the remaining 1 teaspoon of hot water only if needed to form a dough ball. The dough ball should not be sticky.

4. Roll out to a ³⁄₁₆-inch thickness (use a light dusting of powdered sugar to cover the counter for rolling if needed). Use a short bubble-tea straw as a cookie cutter to form the mints. Use a wooden apple stick to push the mints out of the straw onto the parchment paper.

5. Make a new dough ball by collecting and rekneading scraps. Repeat step 4 until all the dough is used.

6. Let the mints dry on the counter for 4 to 8 hours.

STORAGE TIP: The longer they dry, the harder the mints will be. Once the candy reaches the desired firmness, package in little tins for easy snacking.

INGREDIENT TIP: Gum paste is made with pasteurized egg whites, confectioners' sugar, and shortening and is typically used by cake decorators to make flowers and other decorations. It's pliable and dough-like when fresh but dries very hard, perfect for what we want for this recipe. It can be found readily online.

Store for as long as desired, as these mints are shelf-stable.

Party Favor Buttermints

PREP TIME: 5 minutes | **WORKING TIME:** 30 minutes | **SETTING TIME:** 12 to 24 hours

YIELD: 1¼ POUNDS

Be warned, these buttermints don't last very long. That's not to say they have a short shelf life. Rather, they simply disappear quickly, whether they're placed on a dessert table, tucked out of the way on a high shelf, or set out just about anywhere, really. My advice? Double the recipe. My love of buttermints can be traced back to my father. It seemed my dad couldn't get enough of these little melt-in-your-mouth mints. I would watch him sneak small handfuls whenever possible while wearing an impish grin.

EQUIPMENT:

- Rimmed baking sheet
- Parchment paper
- Standing mixer with medium bowl and paddle attachment
- Pizza cutter or knife

½ cup (113 grams) butter, at room temperature

4¼ cups (484 grams) powdered sugar, divided

2 tablespoons (30 grams) heavy whipping cream

1 teaspoon (5 grams) peppermint extract

1 to 3 drops food coloring (optional)

1. Line a rimmed baking sheet with parchment paper. Set aside.

2. Using a standing mixer, beat the butter until creamy. Slowly mix in 4 cups of powdered sugar and the cream, peppermint extract, and food coloring (if using) on low speed. Once all the ingredients are mixed in, turn the mixer up to medium-high. Beat for 1 to 2 minutes, or until the mixture is smooth and creamy.

3. Turn the dough out onto the counter. Knead more powdered sugar in by hand if it is very sticky. If the dough is too soft to work with, refrigerate until firm. Roll small sections of dough into ⅓-inch-thick balls with your fingertips. Alternatively, roll the dough out into several logs of ¼- to ½-inch thickness and use a pizza cutter or knife to cut into small ½-inch-thick pillows.

4. Place the mints on the rimmed baking sheet lined with parchment paper and leave out to dry overnight, or dry out in a barely warm oven for 4 hours (turn the oven on at the lowest setting for 15 minutes and then turn the oven off before putting the mints in).

GIFTING TIP: Make these 1 to 2 weeks ahead of time for your party or event. Make party favors by filling little glass jars or baggies tied with a pretty ribbon.

Store at room temperature in a dry place for up to 3 weeks.

Peppermint Patties

PREP TIME: 5 minutes | **WORKING TIME:** 45 minutes | **SETTING TIME:** 15 minutes

YIELD: 2 POUNDS

As a kid, if you told me that making peppermint patties required sending dogsled expeditions to the North Pole for special snow mint, I would have believed you. The cool burst of intense peppermint encased in a thin shell of rich dark chocolate contains so much wintery essence, the explanation would have been perfectly believable!

EQUIPMENT:

- Standing mixer with medium bowl and paddle attachment, or hand beater
- Plastic wrap
- Rolling pin
- Round cookie cutter
- Parchment paper
- Medium glass mixing bowl
- Stir stick
- 3-prong dipping fork

3 cups (350 grams) powdered sugar

2 tablespoons (40 grams) glucose

2 tablespoons (30 grams) heavy whipping cream

1 tablespoon (4 grams) peppermint extract

1 teaspoon (3 grams) vanilla extract

1 tablespoon (15 grams) butter, at room temperature

16 ounces (454 grams) dark chocolate

1. Using a mixer, beat together the powdered sugar, glucose, heavy cream, peppermint extract, vanilla, and butter on low speed. Once the mixture is combined well, increase the speed to medium-high for 1 minute. The mixture should look like a dough, firm but pliable, not sticky. If the dough is sticky, work in more powdered sugar.

2. Wrap the dough ball in plastic wrap and place it in the refrigerator for 15 to 20 minutes, or until firm enough to roll out.

3. Roll out half of the dough ball to the desired thickness, ideally around ⅛ inch to ¼ inch thick. Use a round cookie cutter with a 1- to 1½-inch diameter to cut out disks. Place the discs on parchment paper and cool in the freezer for 15 minutes.

4. Collect the scrap dough pieces and form into a ball. Repeat step 3 until all the dough is used up.

5. Temper the dark chocolate using the method on page 32.

6. Dip each disk in the tempered dark chocolate using a three-prong dipping fork and place on a second piece of parchment paper. Once the chocolate is fully set, 10 to 15 minutes, transfer to a serving plate or pack in decorative tins for gift-giving.

Store up to 3 weeks in a cool, dry place.

Pixie Sticks

PREP TIME: 5 minutes | WORKING TIME: 15 minutes

YIELD: ⅙ POUND

Pixie sticks are not messing around. You have a sugar craving . . . BAM, the pixie stick smashes it. Simple as that. While that kind of power may seem like ancient woodland magic, it's not. Pixie sticks, the fastest sugar delivery system on earth, are just another example of good old-fashioned American ingenuity.

EQUIPMENT:

- Paper straws
- Food processor or mortar and pestle
- Funnel or paper cone

INGREDIENT TIP: Dextrose is a superfine sugar. It's easy to find online, but you can make a close substitute by pulsing sugar in a blender for a minute. I recommend only making these on drier days, as humidity will make the superfine sugar clump.

¼ cup (5 grams) freeze-dried strawberries

½ cup (100 grams) dextrose

Pinch citric acid

1. Crimp, fold down, or twist one end of each of the paper straws. Set aside.

2. Reduce the freeze-dried strawberries to a powder by pulsing in a food processor. This can also be done by hand using a mortar and pestle.

3. Mix together the powdered strawberries, dextrose, and citric acid in a food processor. Pulse until mixed well. Alternatively, add them to a freezer bag. Seal well and shake vigorously to mix.

4. Using a funnel, carefully fill the paper straws with the pixie dust mixture. Crimp or twist the end to seal each straw.

Resist your inner child's desire to eat them all right now! Instead, store the filled straws in sealed gallon-size freezer bags until the party starts or the urge to have one grows too strong to resist.

Marzipan Apples

PREP TIME: 5 minutes | **WORKING TIME:** 30 minutes | **SETTING TIME:** 8 hours

YIELD: 1½ POUNDS

Ever find yourself envious of Ms. Pac-Man? The way she busts through that video game labyrinth on a mission to consume every glittering piece of fruit, desperate for a few precious moments of total invincibility? If so, these little marzipan treats are the closest thing to a live-action version of the game. First, you make the marzipan bright and zingy colors with food coloring. Next, you form the almond dough into tiny fruit—cherries, apples, pears, whatever. Then . . . get chomping!

EQUIPMENT:

- Blender or food processor
- Plastic wrap
- Gloves
- Rolling pin
- Knife or small leaf-shaped cookie cutter

2¾ cups (343 grams) powdered sugar, divided, plus more as needed

2½ cups (285 grams) finely ground blanched almond flour

¾ cup (220 grams) glucose

1 teaspoon (2 grams) rose water or orange flavoring (optional)

5 to 10 drops red food coloring

5 to 10 drops green food coloring

5 to 10 drops brown food coloring

1. Combine 2½ cups of powdered sugar and the almond flour in a blender or food processor. Slowly mix in the glucose and flavoring (if using) and pulse until a dough is formed. Remove from the blender. This process can be done in a bowl by hand instead, but it will take a lot more time to get the same consistency.

2. Form the dough into a ball. If it is too soft to work with, cover fully with plastic wrap and chill it in the refrigerator until firm.

CONTINUED»

INGREDIENT TIP:
Because traditional marzipan has rose water or an orange flavoring added, I included the option for traditionalists. Feel free to leave it out.

3. Separate the marzipan into 2 large and 1 small dough balls. Put on gloves. Add 5 to 10 drops of red food coloring to one of the large dough balls and knead the color into the ball until the dough is one solid color. Add more powdered sugar if the marzipan is wet or sticky. Repeat with the other large dough ball using green food coloring. Mix the brown food coloring into the small dough ball and knead to make a unified color. Wrap all the dough balls in plastic wrap when not using to keep the marzipan from drying out.

4. Use the remaining ¼ cup of powdered sugar on the counter if needed to reduce sticking, and roll out the brown marzipan very thin to make toothpick-like stems and to cut out leaves with a knife or small leaf-shaped cookie cutter.

5. Roll 1-inch balls out of the red marzipan. Use your fingertip to indent the top and bottom of each ball so that it mimics the shape of a small apple. Repeat using the green marzipan.

6. Add the brown marzipan stems and leaves to decorate the red and green apples.

SERVING TIP: Serve these adorable marzipan candy apples on a tray by themselves or use them as decorations on a cake.

Store finished marzipan apples in an airtight container up to 1 month in the refrigerator.

No-Cook Candy Corn

PREP TIME: 5 minutes | **WORKING TIME:** 45 minutes | **SETTING TIME:** 8 to 12 hours

YIELD: 1¼ POUNDS

Candy corn season comes but once a year. It's a monstrously good time. Don't waste it with the waxy, tasteless orange blobs you've settled for your whole life. Whip up a batch of no-cook candy corn and show the world, or at least the kids who come trick-or-treating, that there's a better way to celebrate their candy harvest this year.

EQUIPMENT:

- Mixer
- Gloves
- Rolling pin
- Pizza cutter or knife
- Ruler
- Parchment paper

⅓ cup (90 grams) glucose

5⅓ tablespoons (75 grams) butter at room temperature

1½ teaspoons (6 grams) vanilla extract

4¼ cups (512 grams) powdered sugar, divided

3 to 5 drops yellow food coloring

3 to 5 drops orange food coloring

1. Mix together the glucose, butter, and vanilla in a mixer on low speed until well combined. Slowly mix in 4 cups of powdered sugar on low speed. Mix at medium-high for 1 minute, or until the mixture resembles a ball of dough.

2. Separate the dough ball into 3 equal sections. Put on gloves and then work (kneading with your hands) 3 to 5 drops of yellow food coloring into one of the dough balls. Repeat the process with the second dough ball using orange food coloring. Leave the third dough ball uncolored.

3. Roll out each ball ¼-inch thick. Cut ¼-inch-wide strips using a pizza cutter or knife. Use a ruler to guide the cuts.

CONTINUED»

4. Place 1 strip of each color together to make flat ribbons of white, orange, and yellow. Push and smooth each layer into the others a bit to make one tricolor ribbon that stays together. Repeat with the remaining strips.

5. Use the pizza cutter or knife to cut triangles in this pattern: /\/\/\/\/\ Repeat with each tricolor ribbon to make individual candies. Place them on parchment paper.

6. Dust with the remaining powdered sugar to keep the candies from sticking to each other, or leave on the counter to dry a bit, turning the candies over occasionally to dry the pieces evenly.

TROUBLESHOOTING TIP: If the strips won't stay together, try wetting the top and bottom of each strip with a slightly damp paper towel to make the strips sticky before pushing them together. Use the least amount of water possible.

Store up to 3 weeks in a cool, dry location.

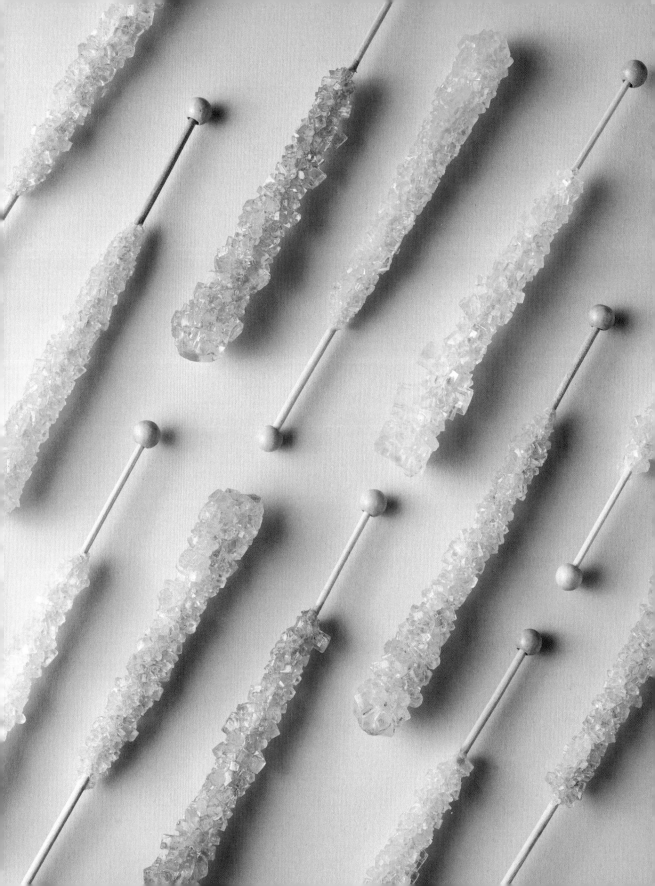

Measurement Conversions

VOLUME EQUIVALENTS (LIQUID)

US STANDARD	US STANDARD (OUNCES)	METRIC (APPROXIMATE)
2 tablespoons	1 fl. oz.	30 mL
¼ cup	2 fl. oz.	60 mL
½ cup	4 fl. oz.	120 mL
1 cup	8 fl. oz.	240 mL
1½ cups	12 fl. oz.	355 mL
2 cups or 1 pint	16 fl. oz.	475 mL
4 cups or 1 quart	32 fl. oz.	1 L
1 gallon	128 fl. oz.	4 L

OVEN TEMPERATURES

FAHRENHEIT (F)	CELSIUS (C) (APPROXIMATE)
250°F	120°C
300°F	150°C
325°F	165°C
350°F	180°C
375°F	190°C
400°F	200°C
425°F	220°C
450°F	230°C

VOLUME EQUIVALENTS (DRY)

US STANDARD	METRIC (APPROXIMATE)
⅛ teaspoon	0.5 mL
¼ teaspoon	1 mL
½ teaspoon	2 mL
¾ teaspoon	4 mL
1 teaspoon	5 mL
1 tablespoon	15 mL
¼ cup	59 mL
⅓ cup	79 mL
½ cup	118 mL
⅔ cup	156 mL
¾ cup	177 mL
1 cup	235 mL
2 cups or 1 pint	475 mL
3 cups	700 mL
4 cups or 1 quart	1 L

WEIGHT EQUIVALENTS

US STANDARD	METRIC (APPROXIMATE)
½ ounce	15 g
1 ounce	30 g
2 ounces	60 g
4 ounces	115 g
8 ounces	225 g
12 ounces	340 g
16 ounces or 1 pound	455 g

Resources

Most of the ingredients in this book can be easily found at your local grocery or craft store. When looking for specialty ingredients and equipment such as lollipop molds, it's easy and convenient to shop online. Amazon is a good bet to find just about everything you'll need. Other good sources include Global Sugar Art, The Baker's Kitchen, and Wilton. For quality chocolate, visit your local chocolatier or order my 1-pound baking blocks online at www.fortechocolates.com. Transfer sheets can be found online at ChefRubber.com and at ChocoTransferSheets.com.

Index

Acknowledgments

A BIG THANK YOU goes out to my Forte kitchen crew for reading and testing all these recipes, especially Julian, who spent many late nights making candy with me, often without warning! Thank you, Taylor, for helping me name Spicy Hog Toffee and for providing me with needed distraction. I also want to thank the awesome people who came out for our 2019 Bike MS: Deception Pass Classic kickoff party and made donations to my team, Forte Farmstrong Heart of Skagit, just for the chance to taste our many test batches.

I couldn't have written this book without the never-ending support of my husband and children, who endured a lot of spastic writing moments and constant survey questions about my candies. Thank you, guys. You are truly amazing!

About the Author

KAREN NEUGEBAUER is the owner and Master Chocolatier of Forte Chocolates, located in Mount Vernon, Washington. Her dedication to hand craftsmanship and achieving unparalleled quality led to a rapid rise in the artisan chocolate industry. An impressive number of her chocolates and confections have earned international awards due to her ability both to master traditional pieces and to create beautiful and innovative flavors. This, coupled with expert tempering knowledge and an excellent palate, is why she is ranked as one of the top 10 chocolatiers in the world by the International Chocolate Awards. Chef Karen serves as a judge for chocolate competitions and consults for the bean-to-bar craft chocolate industry in the United States and Brazil. When she isn't busy crafting amazing chocolates, you can find her spending time with her husband and five children, drawing, or riding her bicycle. To learn more, visit her website at www.fortechocolates.com and follow her at www.instagram.com/fortechocolates.